*Raising A Teenager*

# Raising A Teenager

*Parents and the Nurturing
of a Decent Human Being*

**Jeanne Elium *&* Don Elium**

CELESTIAL ARTS
Berkeley

Published in the United States by Celestial Arts, an imprint of the
Crown Publishing Group, a division of Random House, Inc., New York.
www.crownpublishing.com
www.tenspeed.com

Celestial Arts and the Celestial Arts colophon are registered trademarks
of Random House, Inc.

The poems that appear on pages 115, 116, 120, and 219-20 are reprinted
by permission of Beacon Press. *The Kabir Book* by Robert Bly. Copyright ©
1971, 1977 by Robert Bly. © by The Seventies Press.

Library of Congress Card Catalog: 99-74255

ISBN-13: 978-0-89087-898-9

Cover design by Noren Schmitt
Back cover photo by Heidi Dunbar
Text composition by Greene Design

First Edition

145066704

*This book is lovingly dedicated to the memory of two fine men:*

*David Hinds, publisher, mentor, friend and Lew Powers, advisor, sage, friend*

# ❦ CONTENTS ❦

## ❧ ACKNOWLEDGMENTS ❧

*With many thanks to Veronica Randall, editorial director
at Celestial Arts, and to our agent, Peter Beren,
for their expertise, wise judgment, energetic work,
and supportive friendship;
and to the hundreds of parents of teenagers who asked
questions and strived to be better parents.*

# Part I:

## Writing as Parents
## and Authors

*Once the realization is accepted that even between the closest of human beings infinite distances continue to exist, a wonderful living side by side can grow up, if they succeed in loving the distance between them which makes it possible for each to see the other whole against the sky.*

—Rainer Maria Rilke, *Letters: 1910-1926*

⇌ JEANNE As we set out to write this book, I ask myself why the idea of adolescence causes such a strong reaction in most people. When I tell other parents the topic of our next book, the reply is always a pleading, "Could I have it now, pleeeease?" Perhaps this response comes from our own memories, on some level, of the feelings of awkwardness, anxiety, confusion, self-doubt, and loneliness we experienced during those years. To parent our own children through this tumultuous time, must we, too, relive those pains? Has our own subsequent journey since puberty yielded us enough wisdom to guide our teens through adolescence unscathed? Is it actually possible to enjoy our children's quantum leap in independence during this new stage of development without feeling a total loss of control? Can we finally put to rest the shame of old embarrassments, unforgiven mistakes, and mishandled relationships that still plague us from our high-school days? Whether or not we are prepared, having a teenager in the house brings to light buried personal issues and family struggles, like lifting old stones and finding a mess of worms beneath their earthy surfaces. All that remains unresolved within us from our own adolescence colors our vision of our teenagers' experiences, reactions, and needs.

To my parenting adventure I bring the unresolved issues of confusing relationships with peers and teachers whose mixed messages led me into emotionally hurtful experiences and deep feelings of isolation and loneliness. Will my awareness that I had no one to confide in or to ask advice from lead me to intrude upon our teenage son's privacy or independent thinking? Or will I leave him to work things out on his own like I had to? My sense of loneliness led me into a whirlwind of relationships and activities that kept me constantly surrounded by people, detached from my own true feelings and needs. Might I be tempted to restrict our teen's activities too much or to push him into relationships too soon, because of my own leftover fears? These personal issues will either give me the insight to be a wise guide or cloud my ability to see who our teenager really is and what he really needs. Since I am working with that valuable tool called hindsight, I hope my experiences enhance my parenting vision, and I can settle somewhere between the extremes of what I think my son should need or do. We cannot help but be influenced by our own past. Our task is to become aware of that influence and set it aside whenever necessary to deal with our teens' lives, clearly and fairly.

Our teenager's world is a very different world than the one I experienced as a teenage girl—a small, conservative, Midwestern town in the nineteen sixties. Although we had our share of fatal car accidents, unplanned pregnancies, shoplifting, alcoholism, cigarette smoking, truancy, and fist fights, students rarely brought knives or guns to school; AIDS was unheard of; and the traffic of crack, smack, and even pot had not yet arrived. Sniffing glue or gasoline was the common way to get high, and a father's liquor cabinet was an easy source for achieving altered states of consciousness. In some ways, I feel ill equipped to guide our teen, because the world seems a much more dangerous place than it used to be, with many more life-altering decisions to make. What if my usually law-abiding teen comes home drunk one night? Or he flat-out refuses to do his homework? Or I find condoms in his underwear drawer? Or he suddenly loses interest in everything that had given him pleasure and starts giving his personal belongings away? Or he tells us he is gay? What do I do?

It is my hope that this book will provide a structure and offer insight about who our teens are at each stage of their adolescent development. We learn where their focus of development is centered, what challenges they are and are not capable of meeting, and what they need to feel loved and a part of our family. It becomes apparent that the needs of our teens change dramatically between ages thirteen and seventeen. This philosophy of development becomes a vessel within which to hold the advice, suggestions, new insights, and guidance we hope will support you in parenting your teenagers. It is my intent that this information will help set parents free from the restricted vision and hidden fears we almost certainly bring with us from our own adolescence and enable us to see our growing children "whole against the sky."

❧ ❧ *DON*

At a recent "Raising A Daughter" workshop, Jeanne and I discussed girls and the teen years. A mother raised her hand with the following question: "How do I get my daughter to tell me the truth about her thoughts and experiences of drugs and sex?" Jeanne responded to her question and then asked, "How old is your daughter?" The mother paused and said, "Well, only three." She shared that she was so worried about the teen years that she wanted to start working now on how to deal with these issues so she would be ready when the time came. This is only one example of the fears we hear from fathers and mothers who prematurely focus on teen issues, while their babies can hardly walk and talk. The adolescent years have elicited such fear in today's parents that many are afraid for their own babies to grow up!

In my work as a therapist and seminar leader, I hear an urgent plea from parents for help, for books, for information, for practical solutions to living with teenagers. A quick survey of a bookstore parenting section shows that most books are guides focusing on infants and younger children. We see this trend ending as the children of baby-boomer parents become teenagers.

Interestingly, the word "teenager" can be traced to the *New York Times*, 1947, where it is known to have first appeared in print as part of an editorial. In our books *Raising A Son* and *Raising A Daughter*, we pinpoint the adolescent years from ages thirteen to eighteen, concluding with young adult issues to age twenty-nine. Prior to 1947, or thereabouts, the teen years meant adulthood for most. In less than a few decades, adolescence has become a thriving industry with many adults reluctant to "grow up." Before 1947, young people between thirteen and eighteen years of age wore adult clothing. Today, adults wear clothes created for a younger and younger market, influenced by the media and fashion industry.

Comedian Bill Cosby said in a graduation speech, "They asked me to say a few words about going out into the world. Here they are: 'Don't go.'" His joke is actually a description of how many of us feel; we still don't want to grow up. We are obsessed with youth; we long for fewer burdens, wishing we could live without the baggage of divorce, addiction, emotional problems, and the inevitable life events that catch up with us through time. Here is my motivation for writing this book:

I strongly believe that ALL parents (and I include myself here) are still psychologically stuck in one or some of the many phases of normal teen development. When our teenage children reach the stages (ages) where we have our own significant unresolved hurt or pain, we become caught in emotions and confusion that we don't understand. We may try to enforce rigid control over our teens, rather than offering guidance and limits. We may go unconscious about the very things we ourselves did or didn't do as a teen and hesitate to see the problem as ours. We may be slow to get outside help, finding out from the police, school, friends, other parents, or relatives that our teen has a secret life that we knew nothing about.

We may ignore our spouses and get caught up in trying to live our teenage dreams through our teenage child. We may have affairs when our oldest son or daughter hits puberty, because our own desires are unfulfilled. We may fail to deal with the issues in our own failing marriages. We may mistakenly believe that our teens are now old enough to take care of themselves, and we resume our full lifestyles, leaving them too much on their own. We may go to a therapist to find out how to get our teens to listen to us, yet refuse to deal with our own depression, grief, addictions, difficult marriages, need for medication, and our own teenage conflicts. I know this is true, because I work with these parents, speak to these parents, and most importantly, am one of these parents. I write this book because I, too, need help. We all need help—for our own selves, our parenting partners, our younger children, *and* our teens. Where do we get it?

First, we must seek support from each other. Parenting in isolation invites a struggle where perhaps no struggle is necessary. Teens have the time to network, and we must create the time to find out what other parents are doing and to join them in finding solutions. Secondly, we must deal with our own personal issues, our marriages, our careers, *and* our teens as a family, seeking professional help when necessary. Thirdly, by understanding the developmental stages of adolescence, we become more able to participate in the lives of our teens and to be there with them as much as we can.

We write this book to offer a guide through teenager territory. This guide, however, does not only propose parenting solutions for the teen years. I hope this book also opens a window to the soul—our unfulfilled desires, likes, and dislikes. Through this window lies hope for our teens and our own selves. Through this window lies the vision of how to turn the curse of having to grow up into a gift. The gift of being grown up is the freedom to create meaning and joy instead of chasing pleasure and avoiding pain. We cannot lead well, if we cannot model. I hope this book offers insight during the tough times. There is much healing, meaning, freedom, fun, and joy—not always pleasurable but often rewarding—awaiting us when we choose to finish up our personal business of growing up. With parents who are striving to heal, a young person will fall, land, and begin to live an earthly life filled with compassion and love.

# ❧ CHAPTER ONE ❧

# What Is A Teenager?

*Don't laugh at youth for his affectations;
he is only trying on one face after another to find
his own.*

—Logan P. Smith

**❧ JEANNE** | It's the smells I notice the most. I remember how delicate the smells were in the baby's room, of sweet powder and freshly washed blankets. Even the diapers had a soft, light smell. And our baby smelled new, warm, dreamy, like clouds would smell, if they did; a scent from another world. Now, the smells around our teen have a heavier quality, take up more space; a rich, damp earthiness, almost too sharp to the senses. The smells of emotions colliding with each other hang thickly like fog, repelling, yet exciting all at the same time. I am reminded of a wet dog, still the same loyal friend, but leaving a trail of acrid dankness behind him. Our friend Carolyn says that her teenage sons' room has that "boy smell!"

**❧ ❧ DON** | It's the mood, the air around them that strikes me so definitely about teenagers. Little ones have sort of a chirpiness about them, almost a bird-like presence that carries them along several feet off the ground in their enthusiasm. Teens literally become heavier, flopping onto the sofa, stomping down the hallway. They don't seem to do it on purpose; they are simply becoming more earth-bound, spend more time on the horizontal. And the air around them becomes thicker, darker, sharper, crackling with something like electricity. A friend and I sat watching a ballgame in the family room when his fourteen-year-old daughter walked in. The room was immediately crowded but not because there were now more people. She was loud and took up space without saying a word. When she left, a presence lingered that said, "I was here!"

## Not Flowers, But Weeds

Adolescence seems to cause most parents more dread, more worry, more loss of self-confidence, and more wonder than any other stage of childhood. Why is this often such a confusing time? Why do so many of us look back on our own teenage years and cringe, thankful that we do not have to live them over again, except through our children's experiences? One answer to these questions lies in our misconception of who our teenagers are or should be.

Parents as gardeners and children as flowers have been popular parenting analogies, ones we ourselves have used in our previous books, and analogies that are quite fitting for the years between birth and twelve. However, seeing our adolescent children as flowers somehow does not ring true. Yes, they are still growing and blooming, still needing proper nourishment, and trimming here and pruning there, but their growth and development have a different quality than the flowering plants of childhood. Their faces no longer search for the sun; their limbs no longer reach skyward. Eugene Schwartz, Waldorf educator, author, and internationally known lecturer, writes of teenagers, "And what of the abnormal, poisonous plant? Here we see a picture of adolescence!" [1] Like weeds, our teens go through a period of growing inward, turning away from the light, seeking to create a space within themselves that clearly says, "This is me!" Like weeds, young teenagers create a private, inner pocket; they turn back upon themselves, rejecting and closing off from what they had previously rejoiced in, withdrawing from the forces of nature that had previously nurtured them. The dilemma for the parent as gardener becomes a process of learning how to care for a weed, when all the experiences we have ever had with weeds propel us to spray them dead, dig them out, and throw them away. Many of us gain a therapeutic satisfaction from digging weeds in our gardens, ridding our flower beds of that gangly plant that refuses to grow like the other flowers; its leaves a little too sharp, its stem a bit too woody, its essence too poisonous. Some days we all feel the urge to yank the teenage weed by the roots, shake some sense into it, and throw it out the window! But the feeding and caring of a teenage weed is a much more delicate bit of gardening. It is native to our family garden, and we are responsible for its care, its well-being, and its development.

## Teenagers Are Not Adults

Another reason the teenage years are so difficult is that culturally it is a relatively new stage of life. The world has not always recognized teenagers as we know them. The phenomenon of adolescence is only about one hundred years old. Even as recently as the 1930s, a young teenager's dress and hairstyle remained juvenile, while an older teen's were strikingly similar to an adult's. The recognized cultural symbols that distinctly separate teens from adults today were then just developing. Up until the last century, boys as young as nine or ten were apprenticed to a craftsman, expected to work from sunup to sundown, learning and plying a trade. Girls as young as twelve or thirteen were given away in marriage to bear children for the rest of their short lives. Both boys and girls were initiated into the adult world seemingly overnight. One day they were children, living and playing among the women; the next day, through the time-honored rituals of their particular cultures, they were permanently inducted into the ranks and responsibilities of adulthood. It was unheard of to be supported by one's parents beyond the age of fourteen. An adult of the nineteenth century would scratch his head in wonder at the seemingly idle years of adolescence when our children voraciously explore the world in search of who they are.

Today's parents face an entirely different series of responsibilities from the parents of yesteryear. Then, a father used his political connections or business acumen to place his son as an apprentice, a page, or possibly a student preparing for life in the Church. Daughters were married to men of suitable social rank and financial matches. Preferences, skills, and talents may have been taken into consideration, but a father's decision concerning a child's future was usually final. Nowadays, the long search for self seems, from a contemporary parent's point of view, to stretch ominously into a distant hereafter. We are required to feed, clothe, listen to, encourage, comfort, make rules, set consequences, follow through, spend money on, endure criticism from, educate, and drive our teenagers everywhere, and when they are old enough, allow them to drive our cars! The transition from childhood to adulthood is unclear, the pathway often treacherous, the results unknown.

> *From the wild, stupid stunts and the hard time I gave my parents, I sometimes wonder how I ever survived my teenage years. I was lucky to keep from doing myself in, but I'm sure my parents often wanted to kill me! How relieved they must be that I have a family and a job of my own now.*
>
> *—Nathan, thirty-one*

Most parents expect the dramatic changes that having a first baby brings to a family. Few of us, however, realize how great the impact of our children turning into teenagers will be. We are shocked. The world of the family we once knew is falling apart. We thought that it would be easier when our children got older. Because they look like adults, we expect them to be more adult, but half the time these capable-looking people are tuned out, clueless, or simply not interested. They need just as much attention and supervision as they did when they were three; the difference being that the three-year-old could be picked up and taken to his room! Now, the only thing keeping our teenage children at home is our relationship with them. Without a sense of loyalty and belonging, some teenagers opt to leave their families and survive surprisingly well on the streets through a series of secret, well-guarded shelters.

> *After two months of wondering where she was, my daughter came home. I was shocked to learn about the rooftop hideaways where ten to twelve kids at a time hang out and sleep, sharing whatever food they can find or steal. She was fairly clean and proud of herself, but she said that she was tired of the struggle and wanted to work things out with us at home.*
>
> *—Jennifer, thirty-nine*

## Under A Critical Eye

Our toddler's "No" phase was a trying time, and we sometimes felt stretched beyond our patience at this little being who wanted to do everything her way. That "No!" however, held less sting than the "No!" from our teenager. This fifteen-year-old "No!" often hits close to the bone; accuses us of flawed thinking; of not being able to understand; of somehow being out of touch with what is REALLY going on; old-fashioned, "for Pete's sakes!" The old saw, "Do as I say, not as I do," does not hold up any-more, and we are held very strictly accountable for what we think, say, and do. There is no leniency in the heart of a teen, and we parents are dissected, keenly examined, and stretched out to dry in the merciless light of the adoles-cent's critical eye. Parents cope best during the teenage years when we are able to separate the process that our children must pass through from our own sense of well-being and accomplishment. They criticize our behavior, point out our weaknesses, and find flaws in our moral val-ues. They poke holes in our thinking, sneer at our solu-tions, and shun our advice. Then they seek out our sup-port, plead for guidance, and are frustrated at our lack of understanding. All of this is part of the teenage tasks that enable our young people to make sense of the world and their place in it. It is not surprising that we are confused from one moment to the next about what our teens need from us.

What is apparent is how extraordinarily important good role modeling becomes during our children's teen years. Whether or not we actually practice the values we claim to uphold dramatically affects our credibility and any influence we hope to have on the opinions, beliefs, and choices our teenagers make. Our sharp-eyed adoles-cents detect even the tiniest incongruities between our beliefs and our behaviors. Do we expect them to tell us the truth when we tell little white lies to friends, co-workers, and family? For example, turning down an invitation by saying we already have plans when we don't, or calling in sick to work, because we would rather play golf that day. Do we insist on our teen's honest behavior, such as returning a found wallet with all of the cash intact, when we cheat on our income taxes or fail to report a mistake made in our favor by a check-out clerk or our bank? Or, do we forbid them to smoke when we ourselves smoke three packs a day? How can we expect our teens to sort through the complex impulses of their burgeoning sexuality, when our own sexual fears, needs, and desires are unconscious or out of control? When our children enter adolescence we are challenged, more than ever, to live our lives the way we want our children to live theirs.

This means that if we smoke a pack a day, but don't want our fourteen-year-old to start, we must set the example and quit! Although it is well known that recovering from nicotine addiction is harder than quitting heroin, it is a matter of life and death—ours and our children's—that we do it. It means that if we reach for a six-pack the minute we get home from work and don't stop until we've demolished it, yet we are terrified of our sixteen-year-old getting behind the wheel after sneaking a beer, we must reconsider our actions. Besides, it is clearly impossible to participate in a coherent family conversation over dinner after a whole bottle of wine, a couple of scotches, or three martinis. It means that if we are engaged in an extramarital affair, but fly into a rage when we find a diaphragm in our daughter's sweater drawer or condoms in our son's gym bag, we must examine the double standard in our value system.

It is crucial to remember that what we do will be reflected back to us by our children. However, it is also important to realize that setting high standards and embodying those standards for our teens will not guarantee good behavior—far from it. But, we have to start somewhere, and teenagers can smell hypocrisy a mile away.

## A Second Birth

Parents of teenagers, take heart! There is hope for us all! These years are not a confusing mess, although it feels that way. Our teens' behavior is not inexplicable, although it looks that way. The teenage years herald the development of a new way of thinking—a second birth. "A second birth?" you may ask. A second birth. Our teenagers' brains are beginning to think in a new way. With the onset of puberty appears a beginning ability to transcend the literal, pictorial thinking of the elementary-school-aged child. Intermittently, young adolescents dip into the clear, unemotional perspective of logical thinking. They suddenly see cause and effect. They notice dichotomies in the thinking and actions of others, especially their parents. They have a new ability to explore ideas developed by others, and they become attached to an ideology and spend endless hours debating its attributes.

*When Jamie began to explore philosophical ideas, I was excited. At last my son and I might share a real interest. What I didn't realize at the time, however, was that his newly developed ideals were based on half-digested and little understood assumptions. When I logically pointed out the holes in his theories, he became offended, sullen, extremely stubborn, and withdrawn. I later understood that his ideas were explorations, tests, of his new, tentative ability to think about the questions of social interaction, societal woes, and human needs. When I assaulted his logic, he felt foolish and embarrassed. We had a much better time of it when I helped him follow his thoughts through to a consequence, a result, a conclusion.*

*—Jeremy, forty-nine*

Our teens are able to follow their own thoughts to conclusion, to plan and to think about the future. When an especially gifted teacher offers just the right invitation, a teen's appetite for learning becomes insatiable. If we wonder why they act so differently, it's because they ARE different.

And yet, just when we thought they could assume more responsibility for themselves, they surprise us by doing something that we consider just plain stupid. How many times have we wondered, "Why in the world did he do that? Wasn't he *thinking*?" Yes, he was thinking but thinking in the way he knows best, developed from an earlier age, between eight and twelve. Knowing, however, that it is his wobbly, teenage *thinking* that steered him off course, we can avoid worrying that he is flawed, that we have done something very wrong in our parenting, or that we failed him in some way. Our teenager is learning how to walk all over again—this time with his brain—and sometimes he will fall down.

> *I came into the kitchen just in time to see black smoke rolling out of the vents in the microwave. Jennie, thirteen, was running around the kitchen, shouting, "Mom, help! Smoke! What shall I do?" I immediately put on oven mitts, opened the microwave, and carried a charred, smelly mess out the back door. After opening the windows and turning on the fans, I asked my distraught daughter how long she had cooked her now crisp lunch. "Twenty-one minutes, just what the box said." We both looked at the directions on the box. "Cook for two and one-half minutes (2½ minutes)," I read aloud. "Oh, I wondered what that 'slash two' meant," she said.*
>
> *—Marianne, forty-six*

To really understand where this new way of thinking comes from, we need to understand how the thinking life develops from the start. From the day of their birth, our children naturally unfold with our guidance to become adults, growing from dependent imitators of others' behaviors to independent thinkers with their own mature beliefs, opinions, and ideas. The three stages of childhood development—the Willing Years (from birth to seven), the Feeling Years (from eight to twelve), and the Thinking Years (from thirteen to nineteen)—build upon each other to bring each girl and boy to his and her full potential as human beings.

Thinking for themselves gives teens freedom, independence, and the capacity to learn responsibility. When we understand the development of the thinking life in the adolescent, we find the kind of love necessary to tend to the spikes and thorns, the stinging comments, the noxious odors, and the seductive beauty inherent in every teen's struggle to give birth to the human soul.

## Recommended Reading

*Oneness and Separateness: From Infant to Individual*, by Louise J. Kaplan, Simon and Schuster, New York, 1978. Brilliantly interpreting the child development theories of Margaret Mahler, this book explores the inner emotions and experiences of the child.

*Lifeways: Working With Family Questions*, by Gudrun Davy and Bons Voors, Hawthorn Press, Gloucestershire, U.K., 1983. This easily read book offers a collection of wonderfully insightful essays about family issues.

*Children Without Childhood: Growing Up Too Fast in the World of Sex and Drugs*, by Marie Winn, Penguin Books, New York, 1983. Provocative and insightful, the disintegration of family life is traced from the 1960s to the present.

*Steiner Education in Theory and Practice*, by Gilbert Childs, Floris Books, Edinburgh, U.K., 1991. Childs offers a clear exploration of the child development theories of Rudolf Steiner, creator of Waldorf education.

## Endnotes

1. Eugene Schwartz, "Adolescence: The Search for the Self," a lecture given at the Austin Waldorf School, Austin, Texas, 22 Sept. 1989, 4.

# CHAPTER TWO

# Where Do Teenagers Come From?

*Our birth is but a sleep and a forgetting;*
*The Soul that rises with us, our life's Star,*
*Hath had elsewhere its setting*
*And cometh from afar:*
*Not in entire forgetfulness,*
*And not in utter nakedness,*
*But trailing clouds of Glory do we come*
*From God, who is our home:*
*Heaven lies about us in our infancy!*

—William Wordsworth

These poetic sentiments from Wordsworth so aptly describe our newborns. But why speak of newborns in a book about teenagers? Because, knowing where we have been often helps us understand where we are now and where we are headed in the future. When our toddler sticks a pin in her nose, it is random behavior, and we understand that she is learning through her body. When she wears a ring in her nose at sixteen, we interpret this as purposeful behavior toward freedom and learning through her mind. Tracking the three stages of development from infant to teenager—Willing, Feeling, and Thinking—we better understand the limitations and skills of our children as they approach this new threshold before them.

## Heaven Lies About Us in Our Infancy

Still accustomed to the tiny space of the womb, infants prefer to be securely wrapped in a soft blanket, protected from harsh light and sudden noise, and held close in our arms. Although their dark eyes seem to take in everything around them, there is a dreaminess to their focus, as though they still see heavenly sights that our earth-bound eyes no longer perceive. Our infants are like seedlings, containing all of the necessary gifts, talents, and resources to grow into human adults. The parent-as-gardener, child-as-seedling analogy may be overused, but the similarities in growth are helpful guidelines in understanding development. There are three unique periods of childhood growth characterized by different ways of thinking, distinct ways of learning, and each requires special parenting skills. *In Between Form and Freedom: A Practical Guide to the Teenage Years*, Waldorf educator and author Betty Staley writes, "The child's thinking is very different in each phase, which means that learning is radically different, depending on the child's age." [1]

The child from birth to seven is indeed like a flower, ever stretching, ever looking upward, ever reaching towards the sun, ever seeking and discovering the new. From ages eight to twelve, the flowerchild develops more complex attributes, learns in more diverse ways, and thinks in more intricate patterns. All of this growth is in preparation for the extremely complex thinking and learning tasks faced by the adolescent.

# THE WILLING YEARS: FROM BIRTH TO SEVEN

Thanks to advances in modern photography, we have all witnessed the slow-motion growth of a flower from seedling to blossom. If we imagine watching an infant grow in the same way, we see similar movements of unfolding and stretching towards sights and sounds, light and air. The tiny fingers uncurl, the bright eyes search for interaction, the chubby legs kick in anticipation of forward motion. Infants and toddlers learn about the world around them through their bodies. They touch, taste, smell, and examine *everything* within their reach and even climb after that bright, precious object we thought was placed out of harm's way! The thinking life during these early years is activated through doing; therefore, the child learns by imitating the behaviors, habits, and activities of those around him. Begin any enticing activity near a group of young children, such as painting a wall, mixing cookie dough, or watering a garden, and they are all soon clamoring to participate. "I make cookies!" "Let me paint!" "I want to water!" "Please, I do it!" they shout. And, it is the *doing* that is important. By doing they become the dough, learning about its consistency and resistance. They watch as the paint flows from the brush and creates color where none was before; actually being the brush and the wall and the color, losing themselves in the process. From a parent's point of view it is easy to forget that to a child, the *process* is everything. It does not enter into a young helper's mind that sweeping the kitchen should end with a clean floor! Oh, no. It is the swish of the broom on tile, the flying dust particles, matching Mom sweep for sweep that is so engaging.

## Learning and Thinking

Learning in these early years is focused within the body through crawling, standing, walking, running, falling, getting up, achieving balance, developing bowel control, and thinking. Thinking is achieved via action: "I walk." "I run." "I fall down!" Learning is facilitated through the imitation of the actions of others. Small children learn to do by following our example.

> *I was surprised, proud, and dismayed to find our three-year-old son perched on the edge of the kitchen counter one morning. Cupboards and drawers were open, contents spilling out onto the floor; several towels lay crumpled among egg shells and sugar; one bowl tilted precariously near the edge with a large whisk dangling on the side. All of this mess vanished the instant I saw my son's face. "Look, Mommy! I'm making brekest, just like you!"*
>
> *—Janelle, twenty-nine*

We are sometimes touched and surprised by our youngsters' sensitivity and depth of insight, and it is easy to forget that they do not have the logical and complicated thinking ability of an older teen or adult. They live in the Here and Now from moment to moment, and their observations are most often imitations of what they hear from us and others around them. We forget that expecting small children to improve their behavior after a long explanation of why it is important to do or to not do something is futile. They stopped listening minutes ago, engrossed in the funny way our lips move when we say our m's or impatiently waiting to wriggle out of our laps to get on to the next discovery. All senses are wide open, soaking in every nuance, every word, every movement in the world around them, and storing them away, waiting and ready to repeat back whenever and wherever the memory bubbles up. Like little monkeys, they watch, listen, and imitate whatever interesting comes their way. Sometimes, to our chagrin, we hear or see ourselves in our child's words or actions. The joke about when five-year-old Lisa was asked by her father to say the blessing at a large family gathering describes this so well. "I don't know what to say, Daddy," she whispered. "Just say what Mommy says," her daddy advised. Lisa bowed her head and prayed, "Dear Lord, why did I invite all these people over for dinner?"

In everyday interactions, we experience the often embarrassing, always astute observations and imitations of our young:

- "Mommy says you should lose some weight," asserts four-year-old Amanda to Grandma.

- "Me and Daddy hates lima beans!" yells five-year-old Mitchell.

- Three-year-old Buddy kicked the cat, just as he had seen his older brother do that morning.

- "Daddy is sad today because his car died," reveals five-year-old Ellie.

- Looking in the mirror, six-year-old Annie puffs out her stomach, pulls it in tight, pats her hips, grimaces, and sighs. Her mother recognizes the gestures as her own.

## Feeling

The feeling life of the young child is slowly evolving but is still in the background of development. It is primal, barely connected to the thinking process at all, and expressed all over the body. Even before an infant is a few weeks old, we begin to distinguish an angry cry from a lonely one, an unhappy cry from a sleepy one, but we are often at a loss to know exactly what it is that our little one feels. We know he or she feels something, however, because we see it. Unlike the often brooding nature of an adolescent that requires dialogue and understanding, emotions pass through children in the willing years swiftly, and then they are ready to move on to the next activity. They spend almost no time thinking about how they feel. **The most**

**common parenting mistake is to ask too many questions of our children during the willing years and not enough questions of our teens during the thinking years.**

> *I was a young child in the 1970s and my parents constantly quizzed me about how I felt. "Are you upset that we are out of milk for your cereal?" they asked. "Yeeeessss," I wailed. "Why did you cry when that dog licked your face?" they questioned. "I don't know," I screamed. "How did you feel when Bobby hit you?" they wondered. "I don't know!" I whimpered. I started questioning my feelings rather than feeling my feelings, to please my parents. As an adult I still experience my feelings with my head rather than trusting my gut! I live always just a little beyond myself, analyzing, cataloging, filing.*
>
> *—Heather, twenty-six*

As children reach six, seven, and eight years of age, the abilities to walk, to speak, and to think carry them into the next phase of development with eager anticipation.

## THE FEELING YEARS: EIGHT TO TWELVE

Growth during the feeling years is more subtle than the rapid development we watched from infant to toddler to preschool child. Now our seedlings are in full bloom, active both within the family and out in the world of school and clubs and sports teams. They are busy with homework, art projects, and ball games. Now they plan their days and expect us to support them by providing food, transportation, and spending money. They like riddles, are fascinated by magic tricks, and industriously build forts and clubhouses. Boys are especially drawn to rough-and-tumble play with adult men, want to know what the rules are, and need firm but kind leaders. Girls want to know how the world works, develop intense and varied relationships, and look to strong, capable adults to introduce them to the wonders of what they can be and do.

During what Rudolf Steiner, Waldorf founder, educator, and philosopher, called "the nine-year change," children in elementary school start to leave the fantasy life of childhood behind them. At this age, they begin to grapple with the here-and-now world of a harder reality that later in adolescence causes great disappointment and disillusionment. Now, however, they struggle with their loss of perfection through anger, impatience, and confusion. Temper tantrums, stomachaches, and nightmares are common.

*Meg loved her homework, seemed always eager to do it when we got home from school. But when she hit eight-and-a-half all that changed. I dreaded the battle to do even a short page of math problems. She'd sit and fret about not being able to do soooo many, and she'd erase and erase until there was a hole in the paper, because the numbers weren't formed exactly right. Then she'd wail that the teacher would "kill her" because the page was so messy! When it came time to do a large project, Meg chose to create a model of a Spanish mission that the class had studied that year. It was developing beautifully until she ran into a problem with the beams. When one would fall out of place, she'd fly into a rage, scream, and want to smash the whole thing flat. Every little obstacle seems to overwhelm her.*  —*Marcia, forty-nine*

## Learning and Thinking

The toddler learned through her physical senses; the older child learns through her feelings. She seeks to understand the world around her through the imagination. Her thoughts and conclusions are pictorial in nature, infused with drama and emotion, and often follow no logical sequence. Stories of adventure, trials of good against evil, and overcoming hardships against great odds inspire her to learn, and as Waldorf educator Betty Staley writes, she develops "a sense for things, rather than an *understanding* of things." [2] Decisions are made on preferences and how one feels in the moment, rather than by using judgment and analysis. Children in the feeling years respond to the character and flavor of something, rather than its anatomical structure. In the early study of weather, for example, a lesson has more meaning when clouds are presented in simile form, such as: "cumulus clouds—like a herd of fleecy-white sheep huddled together," rather than as: "a visible collection of particles of condensed hydrogen and oxygen." The scientific description is more easily grasped and understood later when the thinking life truly begins to develop.

We catch a glimpse of this process when our eleven-year-old son laments, "But I'm the *only* one in the class who hasn't seen *Godzilla*!" Or when our twelve-year-old daughter announces that her entire life will be ruined if she is not allowed to go to the sleep-over dance party at so-and-so's house. Our preteens respond to situations with either sympathy or antipathy, rather than with critical judgment. The story about a twelve-year-old with an elderly, ailing dog reminds us of this tendency. Ralphie had been with the family even before Jason's birth and was much loved by everyone. When he lost the use of his hind legs, the veterinarian was reluctant to make a diagnosis without running tests that would cost over four hundred dollars. Understandably, Jason's parents were hesitant to spend so much money because Ralphie was so old. Just as understandably, Jason was set to do anything possible to make his dog well because he loved Ralphie so much. No amount of explaining by his parents could help Jason really understand that Ralphie was too old to ever be well again.

## Feeling

During these middle years, the soul, that part of us that holds our aliveness, begins to develop. If we observe carefully, we are able to catch glimpses of the soul as expressed in our child's likes and dislikes, preferences and choices. We learn to know who he is through his loves and hates, his "yeses" and "nos." But these discoveries often overwhelm both parent and teen, as he reacts differently from one moment to the next. It is not uncommon to watch a student feel remorse and embarrassment following a teacher's reprimand, and a few minutes later the same student is laughing with friends out on the playground. At home the mood changes can be quite confusing: one minute a parent tries to comfort a tearful daughter only to discover that she feels fine after a phone call from a girlfriend. These ups and downs leave us hurt or bewildered, unsure of how to respond to this roller-coaster ride of preadolescent drama. If we use the social interactive style we employed when our child was six, we meet heavy sarcasm dripping with disgust. If we approach in a more adult manner, we encounter confusion or even open rebellion.

Children outgrow their clothes and insist on wearing the latest fashions. All-pink frills that she loved at age five are disgusting to a black-loving teen at age fourteen. Like this natural process, teenagers require age-appropriate responses from parents that meet the teen where she is in the present moment. Staying in tune with the teen's changing needs enables parents to more easily relate to this private world that is developing; a world of grand images, brave deeds, and loyal friendships. The child's external world rarely reflects these glorious, internal pictures, and the development of secrets protects the preteen from public ridicule and disappointment. Slowly, the inner and outer worlds are reconciled, and the child learns to negotiate between the two.

*When I divorced, I was dismayed and surprised by the differences in my two daughters' responses. My seventeen-year-old said, "It's about time you and Dad split. You've both been unhappy for years." My eleven-year-old's thinking was in a different vein. She fantasized ways to bring her father and me together in a romantic setting where we would instantly fall in love again and live happily ever after. In her imagination, she would be the cherished child, responsible for saving our family.*

*—Eileen, forty-five*

This mother will respond differently to each daughter. Her younger daughter needs to be reassured that her mother and father both love her no matter what happens to the marriage and that she is in no way responsible for the good—or bad—feelings between her parents. The seventeen-year-old daughter's thinking, observing, and communicating skills are more developed, and the mother's age-appropriate responses will invite the daughter to share why she came to the conclusions she did, how she feels about the divorce, and what concerns she might have about the family's future. Here is another example:

*Although our sons are three years apart in age, their lives often parallel each other, but I never fail to be amazed at how differently they cope and think about things. Kevin, our thirteen-year-old, was recently left out of a party given by one of the girls in his class, a girl he particularly likes. In his very emotional way, he took this rejection personally, saying that he was ugly and stupid and how could anyone ever invite him to a party anyway! He saw himself at fault. Then, he turned around and decided that the girl was ugly and stupid and that he wouldn't want to go to any parties she had. Jake, on the other hand, sixteen, recently lost his girlfriend, and although he felt badly, he was philosophical about it all. "I really don't want to talk about it. It's over."*

*—Jonathan, forty-five*

This father understood the unique pain of both ages and consoled his sons individually. He allowed the younger one to rant and rave but never gave in to his poor attitude, encouraging him out of his bad moods by engaging him in activities that he excelled in. He also arranged for his son to spend lots of time with his close friends and continuously acknowledged his positive qualities, knowing he needed a change in focus. To his older son, this father said, "I remember when I lost my first girlfriend. I felt pretty bad. If you want to talk about it, I'm here." The sixteen-year-old maintained that it was past him, sulked around the house for several days, then became interested in a school project. Although the younger son reacted more emotionally, both boys felt deeply about these events. The older son, because of his developmental stage, was able to experience his emotions through the insight of critical thinking, whereas the younger son was still in the throes of feeling.

A child's soul is formed as she nears the end of the feeling years. She has a distinct individuality, and the habits, temperaments, and attitudes with which she meets challenges are clearly visible. He often holds a startlingly clear definition of himself, and his finesse at social interaction carries him into the next phase of his development when every skill gets turned upside down.

Thus, it is a slow, gradual process of awakening that prepares the child for adulthood. The physical mastery of the willing years, from birth to age seven, supports the growth of complex feelings. The development of the feeling life from eight to twelve opens the way for turning the key to an adolescent's independence and freedom: the thinking life.

The years between twelve and twenty-one involve a series of initiations that advance our teens toward the completion of childhood. There are three phases in this series of modern initiations into adulthood: The Falling, The Landing, and The Living in earthly life. As we explore these three phases, we gain a greater understanding of the mysterious rites, the curious alliances, and the convoluted reasoning of teen culture. Although it is a culture that looks remarkably different from generation to generation, it is shaped by the same universal human needs: the desire to become a unique self; the need to belong to something greater than one's self; the drive to find meaningful work; and the wish to love and be loved. By looking at the world from a teen's eye view, we begin to have more empathy for the fascination with death, adolescent crushes, the longing to belong, body ornamentation, mood swings, and the wavering between wanting to be taken care of and wanting to be treated as an adult.

## Recommended Reading

*Between Form and Freedom: A Practical Guide to the Teenage Years*, by Betty Staley, Hawthorn Press, Stroud, U.K., 1988. The nature of adolescence from a Waldorf perspective is explored with warmth and compassion.

*Thirteen to Nineteen: Discovering the Light*, by Julian Sleigh, Floris Books, Edinburgh, U.K., 1982. Parents will relate to this personal discussion of the narrowing down of options as adulthood approaches.

*Raising A Son: Parents and the Making of a Healthy Man*, by Don Elium and Jeanne Elium, Celestial Arts, Berkeley, CA, revised ed., 1996. This book includes information about the specific needs and development of boys.

*Raising A Daughter: Parents and the Awakening of a Healthy Woman*, by Jeanne Elium and Don Elium, Celestial Arts, Berkeley, CA, 1994. A specific guide about the unique needs of girls, this book offers recent research and new, feminine developmental theory.

## ENDNOTES

1. Betty Staley, *Between Form and Freedom: A Practical Guide to the Teenage Years* (Stroud, Gloucester, UK: Hawthorn Press, 1988), 3.

2. Ibid., 5.

# Part II:

## The Falling Years— From Twelve to Fifteen

*The rabbit-hole . . . dipped suddenly down, so suddenly that Alice had not a moment to think about stopping herself before she found herself falling down . . . . First she tried to look down and make out what she was coming to, but it was too dark to see anything . . . .*

—Lewis Carroll, *Alice in Wonderland*

From the ages of twelve to fifteen, the young teen reminds us of the two-year-old, his mouth a perpetual pout, arms folded, the attitude of a defiant, definite, continuous "No!" This first phase of adolescence, called The Falling or Negation stage, is often the most difficult for parents when, like the two-year-old, the young adolescent develops a blanket "No" to everything. Many parents say, "Oh, I know the 'twos'. This is easy; I can handle a two-year-old!" Such a behavioral reversal in our teen is deceptive, however. The two-year-old instinctively says "No," because it is part of the developmental stage that consumes him; the willing years when he learns the lessons of the will and the body. He says "No"; it sets him apart; but he doesn't know why. We deal with him by setting strict limits, by putting him down for a nap when he is too tired to handle his emotions, by distracting him with an alluring toy, or by scooping him up in our arms and taking him off to the park for a swing. Unlike our two-year-old, the teenager knows why he says "No" and usually gives perfectly rational reasons for it. His tolerance for physical touch is limited to a swift kiss on the cheek; the suggestion of a nap is offensive; and he is no longer easily distracted by games or toys. He feels the archetypal urge to become separate and unique, and it will not let him go. Whether he is two or twelve, this necessary negation phase sets the child apart and helps create a tangible space in which to develop a separate self. It is as though the child at two and again between twelve and fifteen must sharply define what is not: "No! This is not me. No! This is not me. No! This is not me," before he can begin the painstaking and arduous process of finding who he really is. It is not the same search, however, and parents must adjust their vision from teenager-acting-like-a-two-year-old to teenager-becoming-a-young-adult. This "No" experience seems necessary before the "Yes" experience of integration and a reaching out to others that comes in the later years of adolescence.

> *She stood defiantly before me, arms crossed over her chest, chin jutted forward, eyes blazing. "No matter what you do to me, I am not going to that Sunday school!" my daughter quietly announced. "No, NO, NO! I don't know anyone there, and besides, the teacher is stupid!" Sensing the awkwardness she felt, I remembered my own worst thirteen-year-old moments in groups of people I didn't know. This was just one of the many ways my daughter was beginning to assert herself in her search to make sense of who she is to become.*
>
> —Nate, thirty-nine

Young teens experience a sense of free-falling through the air, afraid, out of control, yet excited all at the same time. They shout "Noooooooooooooooooo!" all the way down, frustrated with their conflicting emotions, awkward body growth, and incomplete thinking patterns. They reach for out-stretched branches, jutting rocks, rope ends—anything to stop this falling. They catch hold of joy only to let go into grief; rejoice in beauty to get stuck in ugliness; fall in love with life then long for death. One minute they are confident and competent; the next minute they are reduced to tears, to a tantrum, or to clinging dependence.

> *Fourteen was absolutely the worst age for my daughter and me. She looked so mature, and we'd have*

*these very adult conversations. Then she'd whine that she couldn't fix her own lunch or go off and do something stupid at school. It was maddening.*

*—Whitney, forty-four*

## A Loosening of the Bonds

During this first phase of adolescence, all of the previous bonds that held the child to childhood become more relaxed. The toddler outgrows the infant who comes "trailing clouds of glory," those filaments of heavenly knowledge. The second-grader shrugs off the comforting caress after a fall. She chooses her own wardrobe. He makes his own social plans. The security of home base no longer acts as a beacon in a storm. The bonds between parent and child stretch to allow room for movement, exploration, and the rise of an expanded vision of self and world. Parental opinions recede in value, while the opinions of peers weigh heavily in important choices and decisions. The young teen hangs suspended over two realities—the familiar security of home and family and the dangerous unknown of the search for self. The spiritual longing that now wells up propels the new adolescent as surely downwards as an apple falls from a tree. As Alice noted, there were ways to distract herself while falling down the rabbit-hole, by talking out loud and such, but really it was simply "Down, down, down. There was nothing else to do . . . ."[1]

### ENDNOTES

1. Lewis Carroll, *Alice's Adventures in Wonderland* (New York: Random House, 1946), 6.

# CHAPTER THREE

# Willing, Feeling, and Thinking—The Falling Years

*Through our great good fortune, in our youth*
*our hearts were touched with fire.*
*It was given to us to learn at the outset that life*
*is a profound and passionate thing.*

—Oliver Wendell Holmes

## WILL AND BODY

The onset of puberty comes slowly for some children and rapidly for others. It is difficult to say why one girl's menstruation begins at twelve and another's after she turns fourteen. Why do some boys' voices begin to crack at eleven and others' at thirteen? Current theories cite nutrition and technological sophistication as influences that determine the beginning of puberty. Many credit the impact of genetics upon the time of maturation. Whatever the reason, a great rush of hormones propels the twelve- to fifteen-year-old into states of fear, physical awkwardness, and social uncertainties previously unknown. This increase in hormone levels in the body alone is enough to send any young teen into a tailspin—and her family along with her.

*Life was moving along fairly comfortably with our twelve-year-old daughter. You know, she came out of her slump over the real world encroaching upon her childhood, and she mastered the skills of sports and music quite well. She had good friends—both boys and girls—and seemed happy at school, although she was sometimes critical of her teacher. Then the bottom just dropped out. She's gained fifteen pounds and wears a size eleven shoe. She doesn't seem to know what her arms and legs are doing. She hasn't had so many accidents since she was two. She's shy and withdrawn a lot of the time, or she's "higher than a kite," flitting from one social outing to another. She doesn't want to do much with the family. Sometimes I don't know how to reach her; to help her be more in touch with what's happening inside of her as well as outside.*

*—Tina, forty-three*

At two years of age, the toddler's body propels him to thoroughly investigate the physical world. He tastes, touches, sniffs, and watches anything within his reach. At the second birth, between twelve and fifteen, the body is again in control, ruled by a dramatic increase in hormone levels. A boy's genitals grow to adult size, ten times the size of the two-year-old. Erections come and go unbidden, causing moments of embarrassed panic. The accumulation of fat on the breasts, thighs, and buttocks in preparation for menstruation affects the body image of countless girls struggling to maintain the cultural preference of thinness.

Like a weed, growth happens quickly: the trunk lengthens; arms and legs seem endless; and feet take on extraordinary proportions. Both girls and boys experience a growth spurt in relation to their own, individual rates of development. Some revel in this new body awareness, constantly testing their physical strength against each other and the odds. Other young teens collapse inwards, folding up upon themselves, trying to make their long limbs less noticeable, their awkwardness less apparent. The developmental phase of puberty creates a paradox. The will of the adolescent screams for recognition and self-hood, while the fear of being seen too clearly in this unseemly body causes them to dive for cover in the current fashion trend: baggy pants, stacked shoes, the color black, pierced body parts, shaved heads, or dyed hair. The young teen craves attention yet fears being noticed. "Look at me! Look at me, but don't look too closely!"

The chemical reaction resulting from the clash of raging hormones and wild emotions causes skin eruptions, increased perspiration, and body odor. Once the vehicle for learning and thinking as a toddler, now the body betrays the teenager. Free physical expression is suspect, no longer innocent. It is not acceptable to cuddle in bed with Mom and Dad or to run naked through the sprinkler. In other cultures we see the automatic greeting of shaking hands or hugging between teenagers. In the United States this form of touch is allowed among girls, but for boys it is more acceptable to punch a friend, perform an intricate handshake ritual, or slap a buddy on the back. One must think twice before draping an arm around a teammate or holding hands with a friend. Teens in the falling years feel physically invincible one moment and strikingly vulnerable the next.

> *Some of my friends' dads got together and cooked up this coming-of-age test they wanted us to go through. We thought it was kinda cool but funny, you know? Like our dads were out to put on this big tribal ritual sort of thing, because we had all turned thirteen. They chose a pretty isolated spot, cooked dinner, told their stories, and then announced that we were all going to spend the night alone, thinking about what it meant to become a man. Some of the guys laughed, but most of us were quiet. This wasn't quite what we had had in mind. You could see the fear in some of our eyes. But, we did it, man! It was one of the hardest nights I've ever spent; creepy noises in the dark, lonely, hungry, tired. But we made it. It felt good!*
>
> *—Mark, thirteen*

## THE FEELING LIFE

Looking again at the development of a child, the infant is strongly connected to the spiritual home from which it came before birth. The baby's eyes are sometimes softly focused, as though watching the "heavenly hosts" fly about its head. Wordsworth said it so beautifully:

*". . . trailing clouds of Glory do we come,*
*From God, who is our home.*
*Heaven lies about us in our infancy."* [1]

As the child grows, she is gradually but inevitably pulled toward the earth, less caught up in the dreamy world of infancy, more attuned to the hard realities of daily life. Between the ages of fourteen and fifteen the feeling life is at its peak, strong preferences and dislikes reign, and the soul forces settle in. The soul is the home of the heart life, and this is where our teenager's passions, talents, and resources lie. These are the strengths that eventually support the will that enables the maturing teen to find and follow her purpose in life. In the meantime, these tender forces stir up a necessary discomfort that encourages the entry into adolescence. On this hard and rapid falling into earthly life, the teenage soul develops a longing, a longing for a spiritual home on earth, for a sense of belonging, for support in creative efforts, for participation in meaningful actions, and for opportunities to serve others.

This deep longing by the young adolescent is predicated on a paradox: while he is still being ruled by his feelings, his faculties for abstract thinking are awakening within. He is learning to distinguish his inner life from the outer world. He is beginning to be able to really *think* about things, but he is still dominated by his feelings. Teens in the falling years look at life through their hearts, searching for beauty, love, cooperation, and community. Sadly, what they often find is ugliness, injustice, anger, and hatred. They discover that life is difficult. Disappointed in what they observe, they experience an isolation and a loneliness that borders on despair. They accept the assumption that life is hard because they are bad. No matter how they try to be good people, difficult or confusing things keep happening. The following story is an extreme example of how despair manifests in the life of a teen in the falling years.

*DON* | At fourteen, Rodney was suicidal and acted out violently at school. In desperation, his parents brought him to me for counseling. The right medication seemed to steady him, and I did all I knew to help him recognize his talents and abilities. Although his situation became more stable, he still thought, "What's the use? I feel better, but I don't want to live." One day I looked him straight in the eyes and said, "Rodney, when a person reaches your age, he has to make a choice. Everyone does. It's like a fork in the road. You have to choose whether to live or to die." When I said the word *die*, Rodney burst into tears. I continued, "People who choose to die, do so because they believe that life is difficult because *they* are bad. They think that if the world would just understand them better and give them a break because they are bad, then life would be a little better." I could see that I had captured Rodney's attention, and I went on. "If you choose to die, you accept the idea that life is difficult because you are bad. And you start finding ways to feel better. You look for pleasure, because it feels good and it helps you forget, for awhile, that life is hard and that you are bad. The trouble is that after you try becoming lost in depression, helplessness, lethargy, and violence, the pain is still there." Never taking his eyes from mine, Rodney asked, "And choosing to live?" **"Choosing to live means that you choose it all.** You accept that you are a good person, no matter what difficulties life brings. You choose to do what has meaning—and it might bring pleasure or pain—but the choice is yours. Choosing what has meaning—what you like to do—always brings joy, whether or not it is difficult. It is a ceaseless choice, life or death." Rodney continued to have problems at school, but he chose to accept life and face the difficulties.

*There's this hole in yourself when you're a teenager, and you look for all sorts of ways and things to fill it up. If you're lucky, like I was, you'll find ways to fill yourself that aren't drugs.*

*—Kellie, nineteen*

This "hole of despair" challenges children in the thirteen-to fifteen-year-old age group to choose life or to choose death. Not the same as the age-old battle between the forces of good and evil, this struggle pits the young adolescent against the belief that "if life is hard, then I must be bad." She must come to understand that she can engage and be active in her life, or she can give up to the despair by becoming lost in drug addiction, computer games, depression, shoplifting, truancy, unprotected sex, and other life-negating activities. Support and reassurance from parents at this consequential crossroads is paramount to a young teen choosing to live over choosing to die. Teens must hear and believe that they are good, whether or not their lives are difficult or conventionally successful.

Parents are commonly mistaken about what support teens now need. We think that our adolescents need self-confidence to successfully survive the teen years, so we continually encourage them to master challenges on their own in order to become competent. We sometimes over-support sports, music lessons, club memberships, volunteer activities, and social events, because we think our teens need these experiences to become self-confident. Self-confidence is indeed important, but at this fork in the road, they need to have a strong sense of self-esteem, to feel worthy as persons, that they are good despite bad things they perceive around them or the struggles they face.

What is the difference between self-confidence and self-esteem? They are closely related but different. Self-esteem is a bottom-line attitude about the self; do I have worth? I am bad. I only cause trouble. No one wants me around. I can't be trusted. These negative beliefs breed inertia and depression. I am worthy of receiving love. I deserve to be listened to. I have a right to take up space. My thoughts, ideas, feelings, and opinions are valuable. These are the beliefs of a healthy person with self-esteem; they nurture high self-confidence. With self-confidence comes the ability to take action, to choose life over self-destruction. Positive action in turn builds self-esteem and a sense of well-being. This cycle is easily interrupted during the teen years, when self-perception is skewed because of confusion and vulnerability. Teens do not often see themselves clearly, and parents can help keep them on track by reassuring them about their self-worth.

*We left Deena in charge of the household and her younger sister for the weekend. She is fourteen, and her grandmother lives just across town, so we thought she could manage. When we returned, the neighbors reported a loud party on Saturday night, and my husband found beer cans in the flower beds. He was enraged, because of course we had outlined the rules—no parties, no company after 8:00 P.M., and so on. During our counseling session, my husband listed all of the things she had done wrong. When Don asked her about it, she said, "Well, I have to correct a few of my dad's points." Don said, "Hold off on that for just a moment. You and your dad could spend the session debating each point, each of you getting angrier and angrier, insisting that the other is wrong. However, I want you to know that I think you are a good person." Deena looked at him in surprise. "You think I'm a good person?" she asked. "Yes, I think you are a good person, who is trying to solve a hard problem." "Then I don't have to refute each of my dad's points," she said. I was amazed at how easily we then talked about what had happened. My husband and I came to realize that Deena was too young to be left with such responsibility, not because she is bad or irresponsible, just because she is young. We worked out a fair consequence, made clearer family rules, and learned how important it is for us to tell Deena that she is a good person, no matter what she sometimes does.*

*—Martha, forty-one*

## Teen Rage

*Dear Mom and Dad,*
*I'm fourteen years old and you're still treating me like the little, snotty-nosed kid you love telling stories about. Well, I'm not that little kid any more, and I hate hearing those stories. You only tell them to embarrass me. How can you know how I feel? You're never around anyway, always working, working, working. I wish you'd just leave me alone, instead of trying to know what I think and do in my spare time. I don't have any spare time; it's all taken up by your stupid rules and chores. You're too lost in your own problems to worry about or even try to understand mine.*

*—Your invisible son who shall remain nameless*

One of the most difficult things for parents to experience is their teenager's rage. "Why is he so angry?" "I don't deserve to be treated that way." "She has such a mouth on her!" "He shows me no respect." "What have I done to make her so hateful?" "After I talk to him, I go to my bedroom and cry." "We work hard to give her whatever she wants, and she treats us like dirt." "We used to be a close family. Now he thinks the world revolves around him." For many of us, rage and anger are not comfortable emotions to feel or to be around. With our teenagers, as it was with our two-year-olds, anger seems to hover, shadowing every interaction. A two-year-old's anger might erupt into violence because he feels all over his body. He kicks, bites, screams, hit his head, and flails at anything nearby. We were astounded at the enormous fury in such a little package. We fear the same will happen when he reaches adolescence. A teen's anger and rage are so near the surface; he looks at us with such disgust; and he is so big. In fact, this age group has the most difficulty with rage erupting into violence.

*I remember the beginning of what happened clearly. I was standing at the sink and Jesse was standing with the refrigerator door open. It was all so innocent. He was drinking from the milk carton, and I said, "Don't do that," and I reached for the carton. He turned towards me, scowling, and the next second we were both on the floor, sitting in a pool of milk, astonished. I jumped to my feet and backed away from him. He scared me to death! My son burst into tears.*

*—Rita, forty-eight*

What is teenage rage all about? When an infant scrunches her eyes, clenches her fists, kicks her legs, turns red and blotchy all over her body, and howls inconsolably, we interpret that she is angry. She feels uncomfortable; perhaps the plastic tape on her diaper is sticking to her back, and a tension builds inside of her, because we cannot find the source of the difficulty. She lets us know in the only way that she can: the tantrum signifies that something is dreadfully wrong, and would we please fix it, NOW! A young teen's rage is also a signal that something is wrong; something is dreadfully wrong inside of him, in other people, and in the world itself. Teenage rage builds during the free-fall to earth, as childhood consciousness is ripped away. Trying to find answers to baffling problems causes rage. Looking for beauty and justice but finding ugliness and prejudice causes rage. Experiencing inconsistency and misunderstanding in family relationships causes rage. Having to face adult trials and responsibilities too early, such as divorce, adult sexuality, and violence, causes rage. Being targeted by the media with claims that all teens have to do to be cool is to buy jeans or smoke cigarettes causes rage. Feeling small but wanting to be independent causes rage. Feeling lonely and isolated causes rage.

The awakening of the thinking life invites an uncompromising attitude in the young adolescent, who so desperately wants to make sense of it all; this sudden growth in the body, these strange shifts in feelings, the unbearable expectations of others, the stresses of performance, the feelings of estrangement from everyone and everything once loved and fulfilling. However, because abstract thinking is new, they cannot make sense of things, and they grasp for something definite to gain some semblance of control. Things MUST be how I expect them to be. Parents MUST still be heroes. Justice MUST reign. Friends MUST be loyal, and so on. When the world does not meet the exact specifications, the only recourse a teen sees is to withdraw, to judge, to feel lonely and isolated, or to act out.

If young teens experience deep hurt repeatedly over a long period of time, their thoughts turn to revenge. Fueled by the belief that "I was badly hurt, because I'm bad," the deep hurt turns into sadness, then fear, then guilt, then shame, and finally anger. Anger fed by deep hurt simmers into angry thoughts against others, name-calling, gossip, and slander. The resulting rage flares into thoughts about revenge until the feelings erupt into action. Although the school shootings in Arkansas and Colorado are an extreme example, these same feelings of humiliation and pain lead to rage and are turned outward; this rage can prompt deeply hurt teens to find a gun. But teens lack the maturity of thinking to visualize and to understand the moral consequences of their actions. For many teens the resulting rage becomes a habitual response.

❧ ❧ *Don* | A fifteen-year-old client of mine explained that he wanted to shock his parents into understanding what he thought about his life at home. "If I was angry, they seemed to listen more. Like, I got their attention, you know? It got to be the only way that we communicated with each other, me shouting and

*DON* knocking things around and them yelling back and ordering me to my room." Sick and tired of the war being fought at home, this young man had finally asked his parents for counseling. During the process, he came to see that his rage had become a habit. His parents, who had been distracted by his rage, learned that their parental commands showed a disrespect that denied their son's new maturity. He no longer complied with their orders, because they were rude. They came to understand how desperately their son wanted their respect, attention, understanding, and involvement in his life.

The rage that our teens feel erupts from a place of longing, of fear, and from the need to grow up. This anger is neither wrong nor morally corrupt. It is a natural response to a feeling that something is changing—painfully. For the most part, this emotion is beyond their control, and they are often as puzzled about these strong feelings as we are.

## The Teenage Crush

During these early years, such feelings of rage and disappointment are necessary. They are part of the falling to earth. It is how the individual self forms. It brings up the "No" that helps a young person sort out what is part of himself from what is not. It is what economist Christopher Budd calls "an emancipation through denial."[2] The teen feels torn apart, shattered by what she hears and observes. To cope with the pain of this disappointment, she seeks out a special friend, a kindred spirit, to help her feel whole again. Helpmates come in many guises: the lead singer of a favorite music group, a popular movie star, an inspiring teacher, a youth group leader, a cute camp counselor, a young, approachable minister, a friend's older brother or sister, or a classmate from school. These "first loves" bloom deeply in the heart of the teen, often reaching disconcerting levels of obsession. Every waking moment is spent in thinking about this person; what he said, or wore, or did; daydreams of being with him, of being loved and sought after. In her obsession and longing for solace, the teen idolizes and projects an archetypal image of perfection upon her crush. The beloved is wise above everyone else, leads the way in personality, can do no wrong. Any outside opinion to the contrary, especially a parental one, is met with disdain and may even fuel the desire to greater intensity.

*When I was fifteen, I fell for this cute guy in junior college. He was different from the boys my age, mature, quiet, foreign. Because he was so much older than I was, my parents wouldn't allow me to see him. I couldn't stop thinking about him, imagining what it would be like to be with him. I planned all kinds of ways to sneak out at night to see him. We'd talk at school between classes, and I finally asked a friend to cover for me by having me spend the night. The date was beyond anything that I had imagined. He was cool, polite, and fun! My parents were furious. They tried to convince me that he was irrespon-*

*sible for seeing me against their wishes, but I didn't*
*care. Then I learned that he dated lots of girls, some*
*even younger than I was. It wasn't until later that I*
*questioned why he saw younger girls rather than*
*friends his own age. In the meantime, it was like the*
*lights went out for me.*

*—Marty, twenty-two*

Most of us remember how bittersweet teenage crushes can be; the exquisite pain of adoration and the inability to own what one desperately desires; the unconscious wish to become lost in the other, to have the emptiness filled, to be consumed, noticed, admired, loved. The importance of the teenage crush is easily missed by parents and others who take these fixations too lightly. "Oh, he's just going through puppy love," we might say, and misunderstand the vital ballast the crush provides our teen during the torturous search for self. The purpose of the crush is to provide assistance in the process of falling to earth; a parachute that helps teens slow and navigate their descent. Their focus on someone adored or admired cushions their fall and captures their attention for a time.

No one is perfect, but when the crush provides a sincere connection and an honest role model for the teenager, his deep hole of longing can be filled with creative acts and meaningful interactions. An admired teacher, for example, who understands the necessity and importance of teenage crushes, challenges the needy freshman to find out about the world through community service, speaking out against injustices, and exploring the ideas and opinions held by those in authority. The teen sits vulnerably in the teacher's power, and the effects of the crush can be either beneficial or harmful.

*As a high school counselor I have watched the drama of teenage crushes. I regret to say that not all teachers handle them honorably. One social studies teacher I remember inspired his classes with his good looks and amusing stories. He was well traveled and gave firsthand accounts of many of the situations and events that were studied. The students responded to his enthusiasm and charm, and many of the girls had crushes on him. One junior had a particularly hard case for him, and she was part of a group who created a special project that involved a sister city in South Africa. The study group spent countless extra hours in communication and the trading of information about the similarities and differences between our city and the South African one. This teacher's time and energy paid off in the deep involvement and learning of these young people. He slipped up, however, with the girl by taking advantage of her adoration for him. He spent too much time and interest in her and when emotions got out of hand, he backed off before damaging his career, leaving the girl feeling painfully hurt and betrayed. It was so bad for her that she left school. Then I lost touch with her. It was very sad, especially because she was*

*talented and bright. Thankfully, the teacher is now a
wiser and more cautious person.*

*—Julie, high school counselor*

We all fear the previous scenario. Most teenagers (and
probably most parents) are confused about romantic first
love and how it is related to sexual awakening. Remembering our own excitement, curiosity, embarrassment, and possible shame about having those first sexual feelings, we may
feel at a loss as to how we can protect our teens from being
taken advantage of or from being sexually involved too
early. Left to the natural inner turmoil and discontent that
is normal for this age group, most teens in the falling years
would be satisfied to hang out with friends of the same sex
or with groups that include both sexes with no expectations
to form couples. However, the pressures from our sexually
permissive society force many young teens to prematurely
navigate the treacherous territory of sexual experimentation. Expected to dress provocatively, girls give uninten-
tional messages of sexual availability, and boys respond
instinctively to any sexual opportunity. In most cases, teens
between thirteen and fifteen prefer the freedom to explore
friendships while dealing with the confusing and even disturbing changes of adolescence without the additional bur-
den of being sexually active before they are ready.

This can be an especially painful time for gay and lesbian teens who do not wholly understand, and may be dis-
turbed and confused by, their sexual urges. Self-hate, feeling alienated, early drug and alcohol use, and suicide

plague the ten percent of teens who are gay and lesbian.[3] Without close parental supervision, direct counsel against sexual activity, and timely, accurate information, the vulnerable teen easily falls beyond the point of no return—no matter his sexual orientation—because of his desires. The feeling life—the life of desires—consumes young teenagers. They do not **have** desires during this phase of development; they **are** their desires. Decision-making, when channeled through these desires, reflects what happens in the moment. Analytical thinking, an ability to foresee outcomes of behavior, is only just beginning and plainly overruled by feelings. No amount of sexual information or admonishment can deter a young couple from becoming sexually involved, if the time and place are right. To develop a healthy sexuality, the best sexual protection for young teens is the close supervision of responsible adults who provide opportunities for safe, fun, and creative interactions with friends of both genders.

Crushes at this age can also take the form of a passion for an ideal, a sport, or an activity, rather than a person. An enlightening portrayal of a beneficial adolescent crush is given in the coming-of-age movie called *Breaking Away*.[4] A love of cycling leads the young protagonist to a fascination with all things Italian, the language, the music, the lifestyle. He channels his qualms about his self-image, his family's social position in a small community, his father's opinions about him, and his future into the challenge of improving his speed and preserving his romantic image of Italian cyclists.

The influence of the peer group on a young teen's perceptions and actions come across clearly in this poignant film. Friends sometimes become a home base, a second family, or the guiding force when one's parents seem uninterested or ineffectual. Whatever a family's stability, consistency, and involvement, however, the support of peers assumes major, even critical, importance.

Meg Gorman, experienced lecturer and beloved Waldorf high school teacher, finds that youngsters who have been educated through the Waldorf educational system support their classmates, are interested in each other's thinking, and proudly acknowledge their accomplishments.[5] She reports that when students from other schools join a class, their cynical thinking is quite contagious, and too many new students hardened by overexposure to a vicious culture can bring the whole class down. The natural desire to learn, to be challenged, and to master difficult subjects is reduced to competition, criticism, and meanness. And a parent's worries about the negative influence of friends are completely justified.

The pressures to be cool drive adolescents in one of two directions. Some compulsively seek friends, often without consciously understanding the attraction or the possible effects of the relationship. Others, failing to find a best friend or clique, become loners, preferring isolation to rejection. Extra attention and support from parents may help the young loner teen find acceptance at home, keeping her sense of self-esteem intact. Most teens eventually find acceptance and a place in their school and social communities. Peer acceptance is vitally important to teens in the falling years, often a lifeline between floundering hopelessly in a sea of insecurity and staying on firm ground.

> *My best friend and I talked on the phone every night after we finished our homework. It didn't matter whether we had just seen each other or whether anything new had happened. We talked about anything and everything for the one hour our parents allowed us. When she was gone on a family trip or to a school event, it felt to me as if a part of me was gone, too. She was my anchor in a really pretty crazy world, and I think I was the same for her. I tested my thoughts against her reactions to make sure that I wasn't crazy, too. I liked what she liked, and our bond grew as we followed the fads from bell-bottoms to disco. To this day I am grateful for her friendship.*
>
> *—Carla, thirty-nine*

But, what do we do when our teens choose friends who lead them into trouble, use drugs, cheat in school, or act out by vandalizing or stealing? Can we tell our kids who they can and cannot befriend? The answer is a resounding, "Yes!" We must know their friends and their friends' families to be able to evaluate this new influence upon our children; whatever the impact, it will be great. Because we cannot (and would not wish to) be with our teens twenty-four hours a day, it is difficult to forbid them to have friends with questionable reputations and expect our rules to stick. Some parents choose this option with varying degrees of success. The following are two very different but extremely effective parental solutions.

Rather than forbid her friendship with a crowd of girls known for shoplifting, Rita's parents outlined the rules and the consequences if she or the girls were caught for any wrongdoing. They told their daughter that if she was anywhere near the trouble, with or without the other girls, she, by herself, would be responsible for paying back the entire cost of the merchandise or for returning it, whether or not the others were held responsible. One day the girl confronted her parents, saying breathlessly, "They are planning to do something, but I left and came home. Really, if they've already done something, I didn't have anything to do with it!" She also announced that she was finding new friends, because it was too much trouble to be involved with this crowd.

A single mother had misgivings about one of her fourteen-year-old son's close friends. Rather than lecturing or demanding he end the friendship, she asked her son about his feelings for this other boy; why he considered him a friend; what he received from the relationship. This conversation opened up a flow of information about the son's longing for his absent father and how important a friend this boy was for him. The mother decided to support the friendship with a few ground rules, to which her son agreed. Until further decisions were made, her son was to spend time with this friend only in their home while she was there. The friend was invited to come over to study, to have dinner, and to watch movies. In the process, the mother got to know the boy better and learned about his family life, developing an empathy and regard for him and an understanding about why her son liked him. This story also has a happy ending for the friend who benefited from the positive inclusion by a concerned family.

## Other Assists

The older generation has always scorned, hated, and mis-understood teenage music. Being part of the former, we admit that we have difficulty appreciating rap music with its monotonous beat and angry lyrics. The appeal of the group called "Marilyn Manson" with messages about death and sex totally mystifies us. We do understand how this painful music soothes our teenager's necessary pain, provides a temporary release from his rage, and reduces the disillusionment endemic to this age.

⋙ ⋙ *DON* When I was fifteen, my dad really tried to under-stand my music. He said, "Now, Son. Tell me what these lyrics mean to you. 'I wanna hold your hand, I wanna hold your hand, I wanna hold your hand, hand, hand, I wanna hold your hand.'" I hadn't really focused on the meaning of the lyrics. I simply felt the satisfying beat of the Beatles' music in my chest, and I was comforted. There was no way I could explain to my dad what that meant to me.

Waldorf educators assert that between age twelve and fifteen is a wonderful time for teens to study the internal combustion engine, because it matches what is happening inside of them.[6] Many art teachers find that when drawing in black and white, making the blacks very, very black emphasizes the white, enabling the young teen to discover the light within the darkness. Drawing skulls and bones channels the rage, tempts death, and defines the hopelessness that teens become lost in. These creative outlets serve as lifelines to hold onto when the descent becomes too painfully rapid. Even computer games such as *Riven*, *Myst*, and *LightHouse* capture the adolescent imagination enough to forget this reality for a time and allow an escape into cyberspace. Without such assists, some adolescents will experiment with drugs or alcohol—anything to numb the feelings, to avoid the pain, to relieve the torture.

## THE THINKING LIFE

The second birth heralds the further development of the intellect. When they feel free to do so without judgment, young teens eagerly engage in thinking, following cause and effect, and puzzling out abstract theories. They often surprise us with their thoughtful observations, insights, and conclusions. Then, they do something that we consider to be remarkably stupid. "Didn't you *think* before you did that?" we ask in desperation. The answer is "Yes," they were thinking, but not in the way that we expected them to. They look so grown up. And sometimes they make very mature statements that indicate mature thinking. Right? But this mature thinking is just beginning to form; it is intermittent, like the first setting on our car's windshield wipers. Swish, swish. Pause. Swish, swish.

Pause. Swish, swish. Pause. Our teen performed that stupid behavior during the Pause. Her thinking then was the thinking she developed during the feeling years—thinking ruled by feeling, more pictorial, less rational than we thought the situation called for, her habitual way of thinking—until now. With the onset of the thinking life that began to change, but she wasn't quite in control yet. Rational thought had not yet become a habit. Swish, swish. Pause. Swish, swish. Pause.

> *My thirteen-year-old son developed a passion for woodworking. I thought this was a great way for us to connect, so I taught him how to use—and take care of—the power tools. He was quite gifted, really, in design and the actual building. He failed miserably at taking care of the tools to the point that I raged at him every weekend. I couldn't understand why he seemed so thoughtful with the project and then totally spaced out when it came to the tools. Leaving the saw out in the rain was the final straw, and I grounded him from the shop. I couldn't understand why he wasn't more responsible with the tools. When I heard the Eliums talk about intermittent thinking in the young teen, I got it. It was as though my son had enough brain power for the project and then his brain automatically switched off for a rest. The tools were just beyond him at that point, so we now either put the tools away together, or I kindly remind him. Knowing that this negligence wasn't intentional took all of the blame out of it for me, and I could deal with*

*my son with a more positive and helpful attitude. It made all the difference in our relationship.*

—*Ben, forty-five*

Swish, swish. Pause. Swish, swish. Pause.

## Thinking and Inner Guidance [7]

Each of us relies on internal guidance that helps us know the truth, choose right action from wrong action, and alerts us to how we feel from moment to moment. Connected to our emotions and feelings, this inner guidance began developing the instant we were born, and we trust or disregard it according to our needs and experiences. For example, a small boy falls off his tricycle and scrapes his knee. His mother tells him that he is not hurt and gently puts him back on his trike. Immediately a confusion sets in. His knee smarts badly, and he would really like to cry from the pain. His mother, however, the person on whom he depends for everything—the person who knows everything—says that it doesn't hurt. Who can he believe? That inner voice that says, "I hurt," or his all-knowing mother? Having this experience repeated over and over in its various scenarios eventually teaches the boy to doubt his own experience and resulting internal wisdom.

Some of us were lucky enough to have parents, or other influential adults, who encouraged us to trust our selves; or we were able to persevere with our own sense of things in the face of outside authority. The voice of inner guidance is a teen's messenger from the soul and carries them through the negation years by expressing likes and dislikes, preferences and antipathies. When thinking, as it is now developing, is linked with these emotions—these likes and dislikes—our adolescents begin to make more enlightened choices. What was mostly reflex in response to feelings during the years from eight to twelve now begins to be thoughtful action. "I really don't like rap. I'm more interested in jazz," observes a fourteen-year-old. This preference is followed by action with an investment in a collection of jazz CDs. In another example, a thirteen-year-old discovers that she doesn't really feel comfortable with children under five years of age. "I prefer baby-sitting jobs with kids between six and ten," she decides.

Like logical thinking, listening to one's inner guidance is sporadic and intermittent. Life experiences bring wisdom to these internal messages, and our teens learn by exploring and trying on various ideas, habits, and opinions. Learning to trust their inner guidance is built like a house, board by board. The involvement of parents and community is crucial in the positive development of teenagers. Parents must develop the patience to allow our teens to "screw up" and start over, to "screw up" and start over, to "screw up" and start over. By setting clear limits and following through on natural consequences, we assist our young teens in hearing their inner guidance, strengthening and honing its responses to help them make the difficult choices they will inevitably face as they search for truth in the outside world.

## Recommended Reading

*Self-Esteem: A Family Affair*, by Jean Illsley Clarke, Hazelden, Center City, MN, 1998. In this new edition, Clarke offers general principles that apply to families with children of all ages.

*Dare to Live: A Guide to the Understanding and Prevention of Teenage Suicide and Depression*, by Michael Miller, Beyond Words, Hillsboro, OR, 1989. From a dynamic presenter, this is an upbeat and practical look at how to recognize and deal with teenage depression and suicidal behavior.

*The Angry Teenager*, by Wm. Lee Carter, Thomas Nelson Publishers, Nashville, TN, 1995. This very helpful guide to dealing with teenage anger helps parents overcome their own anxieties and fears.

*Ask Me If I Care*, by Nancy Rubin, Ten Speed Press, Berkeley, CA, 1994. The strong feelings and opinions of teenagers come through loud and clear in this poignant collection of adolescent writings.

*The What's Happening to My Body Book for Girls* and *The What's Happening to My Body Book for Boys*, by Lynda Madaras, Newmarket Press, New York, 1988. These guides are great for parents and young teens to read together and discuss.

*Homosexuality: The Secret a Child Dare Not Tell*, by Mary Ann Cantwell, Rafael Press, San Rafael, CA, 1996. This insightful book helps parents understand and deal with the complicated feelings and issues of gay and lesbian children.

*Children the Challenge*, by Rudolf Driekurs, E.P. Dutton, New York, 1964. Driekurs guides parents to find that difficult balance between letting children run wild and stifling them.

## ENDNOTES

1. William Wordsworth, "Intimations of Immortality from Recollections of Early Childhood," *The Poetical Works of Wordsworth*, Cambridge ed. (Boston: Houghton Mifflin, 1982), 354.

2. Schwartz, *Adolescence*, 15.

3. Suicide Information and Education Center in Canada, (403)245-3900, www.siec.ca and Parents and Friends of Lesbians and Gays (PFLAG), www.pflag.org\pom\teen.html.

4. Peter Yates, director, *Breaking Away*, Fox Productions, 1979.

5. Meg Gorman, in a parent discussion group about adolescents, East Bay Waldorf School, El Sobrante, CA, Spring 1998.

6. Gorman, lecture.

7. In our previous books, we refer to an internal guidance as the *inner guidance system*. Because our views encompass a holistic perspective, rather than a mechanistic one, we now call this internal voice of wisdom, *inner guidance*.

# CHAPTER FOUR

# Fences for the Falling Years

*Youth, which is forgiven everything,*
*forgives itself nothing…*

—George Bernard Shaw

The purpose of the garden fence is not to punish the flowers but to protect them from four-legged nibblers seeking out the first tender buds. The purpose of family rules, limits, boundaries, and consequences is to keep our children safe and to help them achieve their own internal self-discipline. Until our children develop an internal sense of morality to guide their behavior, parents must be their leaders, erecting fences that give them a safe place to grow and lighting beacons to show them appropriate conduct. When our little ones were under seven, we literally erected fences they could not climb over—cribs, door gates, and garden walls. With strict enforcement and our constant presence, we gave admonishments and set rules to keep them safe: "Don't touch. It's hot!" "Hold my hand while we cross the street." "Don't eat the berries!" and so on. As they grow, these rules become part of their inner guidance, helping them make safe behavior choices. Eventually, our rules become more sophisticated, with agreements from our children and gentle reminders from us: "Today is trash day. Be sure to put the bin near the curb." "Please gather your dirty clothes and take them to the washing machine." "When you get to Suzy's house, please call to let me know that you got there safely." And so on.

When our children become teenagers, their loyalty and commitment as family members decrease, and they become less willing to cooperate in family chores or follow family rules. Like contrary yearling colts, they begin to lean against or leap over fences built to keep them safe. Their drive to grow up pushes them toward greener, broader pastures. No longer are they dependent upon us for their well-being and sustenance, for they have the resources to take care of themselves and to survive on their own.

*I look at Scott and realize that at fourteen the only thing keeping him here at home is his relationship with us. He tells me about the shelters where guys in his high school stay when their parents kick them out. Our commitment to spending time together as a family has really paid off, because even when he is in one of his "moods," there's a deep heart connection we share. We've developed a bond that goes beyond his anger and confusion. Knowing that he can count on our support and our holding firm on rules seems to keep him anchored amidst all his teenage angst.*

*—Bette, fifty*

The potential violence that punctuates the teenage years causes many parents to throw up their hands in submission. "Okay! Okay! We give in. Have your own way about it. There's nothing we can do to stop you from doing (whatever) if you're that determined." But without close parental involvement, the fences that keep them safe and help guide their behavior fall into disrepair, and may even be torn down. Teenagers in the falling years are particularly vulnerable to violent feelings as they plummet to earth. This frightening journey can create intense feelings of alienation, awkwardness, loneliness, and, ultimately, abandonment and can manifest as anger, cynicism, sarcasm, and hopelessness. Without firm limits, teens flounder in confusion and their revenge on us may manifest as risk-taking, or a reckless disregard for themselves or others. Now they face the greatest risk of suicide, accidents, drug use, eating disorders, unplanned sexual activity, and problems at school.

> *"Most childhood misbehavior . . . is not the direct result of inherited rottenness; diseases of the mind or body; social or economic woes; television, movies, and rock music; or other situations beyond parental control. A child's misbehavior is simply an exercise of power—doing what he or she wants to do in the absence of active parental authority."* [1]
>
> —*Gregory Bodenhamer, Cofounder of the* Back in Control *program*

# Parent Power

*JEANNE* | I had to unlearn many unhelpful parenting habits picked up from my generation's idea of democratic child-rearing. For example:

- We shouldn't be too strict for fear our children will rebel against harsh rules.

- We must consider their desires because we must not infringe upon their individual rights.

- We must offer them numerous choices so they feel a part of the family.

- We must explain our reasons for saying "Yes" or "No," so they will understand and therefore be more willing to accept our decisions.

- We must be polite so they will follow our example.

- Our children must like us, so we must strive to be good buddies, always open, fair, and kind.

This style of democratic parenting does not grow responsible, dependable, cooperative children. Instead, it creates angry, confused, and frustrated parents, crippled by the concept that freedom makes families work. We get sucked into arguments with our teens that deflect us from the real issues at hand. We feel guilty when they fear being left out, claiming that "everyone else is doing it!" We worry that our rules are unfair or too tough; that life is too hard, that the consequences of their behavior are too stressful for them to face; that we may damage their self-esteem. We are not even sure that we have the right to demand certain behaviors from our teens! They present such a determined front—the determination to be in control; to run their own lives; to experience the world on their own terms.

This determination to run their own lives is a healthy sign that our children are growing up. However, **they are not yet ready to experience the world on their own terms.** The truth is that our teens need fences now just as much or more than they did when they were toddlers. Their determination to be individual and independent is only inches deep. They crave to belong—just notice how much they and their friends dress and act alike. Their deep longing to be part of a group leaves young adolescents vulnerable to the pressures of their peers to engage in activities beyond their maturity. Most of us wonder how to help our teens find their way through the maze of temptations: smoking, drinking, drugs, sexual activity, reckless driving, stealing, vandalism, and so on. One mother of teenage boys says, "The only way to help them through these treacherous years is to stay right in their faces!" Although they may openly disparage us, they need our attention, feedback, encouragement, and involvement in their lives. It is easy to lose track of who they are; our lives are so busy and their lives have become so much more complex.

*It wasn't until I slowed down and really noticed what my son was doing that I saw how things just didn't add up. The extra cash he always seemed to have I had assumed was birthday money. He'd spent that long ago. The new computer, CD player, and skateboard I thought his dad had given him were simply too costly for his dad to afford. The lock on his door and his offer to clean his room made me think that maybe he was growing up and accepting more responsibility for himself. He was actually hiding the stash of marijuana that he dealt regularly to friends at school. He had created an entire life that I knew nothing about! I was stunned!*

*—Sandy, mother of Stan, fourteen*

The solution for this family was long and agonizing. Once a teen has developed a secret life, the way home again is not a simple one. This mother had to face the reality of the situation: her son was not only a drug user, but a pusher. First of all, she apologized to her son for not being more involved in his life and told him that this was going to change. She made appointments with each of his teachers to check on his school performance and to let them know that she was becoming more involved in his academic progress. She requested a phone call when anything seemed irregular. She called the parents of each of her son's friends just to say that she was keeping in closer contact with her son and asked for their support. Then, she removed the door to her son's room. She told him that he had lost the privilege of privacy, because he had broken the house rules about drugs. She restated the rules that drugs were not allowed in the house, in the car, or hidden in clothes and belongings. With her son's help, she cleaned out his room, flushing the drugs down the toilet and donating his new acquisitions—the computer, CD player, and skateboard—to a local charity. She told her son that she would be conducting unannounced weekly room checks and locker checks to make sure that everything was clean. She offered him a way to earn money to save for the things he had given up. She also arranged with family members to help supervise her son during the after-school hours when she worked. This mother also attended educational classes at a local drug rehabilitation treatment center.

For several months, life seemed to settle down for this mother and teenage son. Then, he ran away. The mother heard from several teachers that he was absent from class. After four days, her son was found staying with a group of college students. She told him, "You can come home when you are willing to follow the new rules AND after you have completed a drug treatment program." Six days later, her son knocked on the door, asked to come in, and told his mother that he had enrolled in a drug program. He promised to go to school and to follow the new rules, if he could come home. After four months of treatment, finding new friends, and getting an after-school job, this teenager is more cooperative at home, doing better in school, and is more affectionate with his mother. She says, "I learned a huge lesson. I thought that I would have more time for my own life when my son became a teenager, but your parenting commitment doesn't lessen at all until they are out on their own. Then? Maybe. I also learned that empty threats have no impact and that I have to have a back-up plan for any rule that I make."

Common misconceptions about teenagers make parenting not only ineffective and misdirected, but punitive and debilitating. For teens in the falling years, fences should be just low enough to allow the freedom of exploration that is so essential for the development of an individual self, and high enough to provide the protection and guidance inherent in facing the confusion and temptations of the modern world.

MISCONCEPTION #1: **The number one most common misconception is to assume that our young teens, because they look older, have the common sense to make more mature choices.**

"She looks like an adult, so she should act (think) like an adult." Remember swish, swish, pause? A teen between twelve and fifteen does what we ask her to do only about one time out of three. We want consistency in behavior and thinking before acting, but our young teen has not yet developed these desirable habits. The maturing of the intellect is just beginning, and the feeling life is at its peak. When we create a situation in which too much is expected, we are often disappointed, and this usually leads to arguments, accusations, and power struggles that result in personal hurt and loss of connection.

◁▷ ◁▷ *DON* Parents who complained that their kids were inconsistent at twelve to fourteen, amazingly report that they are suddenly more reliable as fifteen- to sixteen-year-olds. It takes about three years to mature enough to be able to be more consistent. But by that time, both teens and parents are black and blue from the struggle.

## Supervision

One of the hardest things to hear about parenting teens between twelve and fifteen is that many of their difficulties arise from lack of close parental supervision. "How can we give more supervision when our lives are so busy?" we wonder. However, when we become too lax in the enforcement of family rules, we lose that precious heart-to-heart connection that keeps our teens safe and involved in family life, a vital anchor in the chaos of adolescence. Close supervision means that we know:

- what they are doing;

- where they are doing it;

- with whom they are doing it;

- they have done their homework;

- they attend class regularly;

- they have appropriate friendships;

- their money is legally earned;

- they take responsibility for household chores;

- and that they take part in family life.

The fine line parents must tread is to provide enough supervision to keep teens safe, while at the same time allowing the privacy required to develop a unique self. Daily involvement with our teens is *required* during the falling years. Mood and situations change so rapidly that no one could possibly stay in touch without setting aside time on a regular basis for conversation and catching up.

*We realized early in Jake's teen years that our busy schedules prevented us from knowing enough about his activities. This was a drastic move, and I know not all parents can do it, but I decided that he needed me at home now as much as he did when he was little. I was lucky enough to be able to change from full-time hours to part-time. Being there when Jake got home from school or driving him and his friends around helped me keep current on interests, activities, and friendships. I often learned the most about his life by quietly driving while he and his friends chatted in the back seat.*

*—Amanda, mother of Jake, thirteen*

*Brad reacted to adolescence by disappearing into his room. The only time we saw him was for family meals, and we made sure that he abided by the rule that we all eat together. It took us awhile to learn how to listen for information about his life, but he opened up to us when we stopped giving advice and criticizing his thoughts and actions. In a school lecture about young teens we heard the magical three little words: "Tell me more." When Brad understood that we really wanted to hear what he had to say without judgment, he came out of his room more often, was a little less gloomy, and was more cooperative around the house.*

*—Daniel, father of Brad, fourteen*

## Simplify, Simplify, Simplify

To get our young teens to do what we ask requires that we request simple tasks and make simple transactions. Avoid making complicated deals. The bargain, "If you empty the trash every day for a month without being asked and without forgetting, you can buy that book you want," is doomed to fail from the start. The agreement is too complicated and too future-oriented for any young teenager. He may perform perfectly for three days but on the fourth, fifth, and sixth days, a new interest supersedes his desire for that book, and he forgets to take out the trash. If we are not there with constant gentle reminders, he fails in his agreement, gets more and more behind, and we are tempted to use guilt or shame to get him back on track. Thus begins the angry-shouting-insulting-hurtful syndrome that is so easy to fall into and so difficult to get out of.

Avoid using the "credit card system" of negotiation. Your teen suggests, "If you give me twenty dollars now for a CD, I'll wash your car for you on Saturday." A more certain approach is to offer, "Wash my car, and I'll pay you five dollars," because by Saturday after the CD is a few days old, the incentive to wash your car is rapidly fading. Not because she is irresponsible, but because she is now concerned with what dress to wear to the prom. Swish, swish, pause. Simplify, simplify, simplify.

**Be clear about acceptable behavior.** Avoid using wishy-washy statements in hopes that teens will make appropriate behavior choices. "Smoking is a disgusting and unhealthy habit. We hope you won't smoke," ineffectively goes up in smoke, so to speak, when your teen is offered a light. The unequivocal statement, "As long as you live at home, you may not smoke," carries much more impact. The teen is held accountable for keeping the family rule of not smoking as long as he is living under the family roof. When he is living on his own, he will decide for himself. The good news is that recent studies indicate that people who make it through the teen years without smoking rarely start the habit as adults.[2]

MISCONCEPTION #2: **The second most common misconception about young teenagers is the notion that if at first they don't succeed, they are utter failures.**

"He had his chance, and he blew it." Again, remember—swish, swish, pause. Teens in the falling years need lots of chances to fail, start over, and try again. These are the years of experimentation. They are fascinated by what works and what doesn't work. They continually search for new ways to do something with their own personal stamp on it. A common parental reaction is a worst-case scenario: "If he can't come home on time for dinner, how will he ever get to work on time when he has a job?" "If he's breaking into soda machines, how long will it take before he's breaking into houses?" "If he carries a knife to school, will he be an ax murderer on death row later on?" Our alarm about his behavior feeds our mistrust and gives birth to poor judgment. We overreact, setting boundaries and consequences that limit movement, shut down communication, and cut off understanding. Our relationship with him becomes a "you vs. us" struggle for power, and we lose the battle before we really start. The stubbornness of young teens is legendary. Their tenacious grasp of the opponent position would put any bulldog to shame.

At heart teenagers want to succeed, and true to the words of British dramatist George Bernard Shaw, they are their own worst critics; they forgive themselves nothing. This perfectionistic urge leads some teens to resort to cheating or lying when faced with the possibility of failure or of being held accountable for their actions.

> *I had straight A's going into the final quarter of my freshman year. I was also on the debating team and played water polo. There was no way I could pass my French test without a miracle. The miracle turned out to be my friend Bob, who, without being caught, managed to give me the answers during the test. I had this*

*bad feeling in my chest during the whole thing, and I couldn't look my mom in the eyes for a week. But I couldn't stop myself. I had to pass that test!*

*—Patrick, fourteen*

*I think I was more shocked at my daughter's lies than with her behavior. I thought we had always been pretty open with each other, and I was certain that she could come to me with any problem. It wasn't until I got my credit card bill that the truth came out. Her mother had helped her shop for her first formal dress for a school dance. I guess they had a pretty ugly disagreement about the kind of dress my daughter wanted—a long, slinky white number that my wife firmly vetoed as too old for her. After giving in to a tamer dress, my daughter decided to take my credit card and go back later for the dress she really wanted, intending to change at the dance and return it afterwards. The glitch in her plan was that at a post-dance party, someone spilled a glass of red wine down the front of the dress. She was in deep trouble with being at the party, drinking wine, taking my credit card, and lying about the source of the charges. She said, "All I could think about was that cool dress and how everyone's eyes would bug out when they saw me in it."*

*—Martin, father of Alicia, fifteen*

Learning to admit, accept, and make amends for their mistakes is a painful process during the falling years. Parents often find it difficult to determine an effective balance between making allowances for their teens because they are young and holding them to a certain high level of achievement. Trying to live up to expectations that are too high force many teens to resort to cheating or lying about their behavior.

## Focus Less on Punishment, More on the Relationship

Effective parents are not evil taskmasters with whip in hand, ready to punish every misdemeanor or correct every underdeveloped theory. We are family leaders, searching for the meaning and positive intent of our adolescent children's behavior and providing direction in the form of family rules to develop their internal guidance. Our leadership encourages and sustains the precious parent-child bond that began in infancy.

**The relationship we foster into the teenage years is what motivates our children to do what we ask them to do, because they trust it to be right.** This relationship, like a tapestry, is composed of many threads, woven together to support the core of who our children are going to become. Through the connection we create with them, their inner guidance is developed and strengthened. Our presence in their lives and the rules and limits that we set are not only to keep our children in control, but to engender their self-confidence to make safe and wise choices. When they are on their own, will they be able to make the choice that is right for them? Within a relationship of respect, kindness, firmness, clear rules, humor, and love, a child feels safe and develops the inner confidence to become self-reliant.

> *My sister and I were an anomaly at our boarding school. We did not participate, as most of our classmates did, in the destructive acting out behavior of teenagers. It was not the fear of being caught that kept us from drugs, drinking, smoking, and sex. It was something much deeper and more subtle. The relationship that our parents created with us for the first thirteen years of our lives instilled an inner knowing that we were just not ready, or really very interested in, those experimental activities. It went beyond that, too. Our parents had shown us so much trust, love, and confidence that we never wanted to do anything that would make them ashamed of us or that would let them down in any way. I don't remember any harsh, definite rules, like, "Don't ever smoke!" or "Never drink." I do remember my folks telling us how fabulous we were, and with that belief, we developed a confidence to make decisions that were right for us, even in the presence of enormous peer pressure.*
>
> *—Ashley, thirty-two*

What if, for some reason, we as parents were unable to develop or keep a strong bond with our children? Is it too late, when they become teenagers and in need of firm guidance, to repair the crack in our relationship? No! It is never to late to try! It takes an enormous amount of humility, patience, forgiveness, and honesty. And help from others. For whatever reason we lost contact with our child—divorce, illness, career priorities, immaturity, imprisonment—there will probably be deep feelings of fear, anger, mistrust, and sadness on both sides. Rebuilding a lost relationship usually takes the help of a skilled and caring professional. An absent parent must find tremendous courage to forgive him- or herself for the failure to be there and to hear the feelings of betrayal experienced by his or her child. To be willing to do this for ourselves, as well as for our children, is one of the greatest gifts they will ever receive.

**Our relationship with our children should nurture a desire to seek understanding in times of trouble rather than blame and accusations.** Because we care, we want to know what motivated our teen's behavior. Knowing leads to understanding, and understanding, we know better how to respond. Why did our son feel that he needed to carry a knife to school? How did he think that robbing a vending machine would solve a problem? Realizing that our four-teen-year-old was late for dinner because he didn't accurately calculate the distance and time it would take to get home, rather than because he was inconsiderate of his family, avoids the trap of moralizing, threats, or punishment. Without a big pep talk, a long lecture, or an involved explanation, calmly say, "Let me help you try again." Rather than accusing him of being irresponsible and uncaring about others, help him do the math: "If you are expected home for dinner by six, and you have a twenty-minute walk from Sam's house, you have to leave by five-forty." Most of all, avoid using "You never . . . ." or "You always . . . .," because it is not true, and he will be hurt and insulted that we do not recognize his efforts.

## Lower the Expectations

For the fourth time this week, we discover the sticky remains of our teenager's snacks between the cushions of the family room couch. He simply cannot remember to return the debris and the dishes to the kitchen when he has finished. "That's it! No more snacks!" we decide, not thinking about the long-term consequences of this declaration. Once we come to our senses, we realize that our expectations were too high. He is not capable of eating in the family room in front of the TV and *always* throwing away the leftovers when he is finished. Many times his mind is not on the snacks, the condition of the couch, or the mess left behind. After his program, he is out the door and on to another fascinating adventure in this game of life. "But he *should* pay more attention; he *should* be able to do this simple task; he *should* be more responsible," we protest. Yes, perhaps he should, but he continues to fail, and most forms of punishment will only create resentment, hostility, and loss of connection rather than obedience to our wishes. Our expectations are too high, and we must bring them down a notch. The family rule for younger children becomes the rule for all children: all snacks are to be eaten at the kitchen table and the dishes put in the sink when finished. This saves the family room couch from an ant invasion and us from the onerous task of standing over our reluctant teen while he cleans up the mess, or of doing it ourselves. He looks old enough, but his failure has proven that he is not yet capable of sharing the right to eat outside the kitchen. We change the expectation to what is doable for now, rather than trying to teach him something that he is not yet able to master. Because of his stage of development—the falling years—he still needs to take baby steps towards assuming adult responsibilities.

*Most arguments with my fourteen-year-old daughter center around the mess she continually leaves around the house. Her homework papers piled on the dining table; sweater left on the floor near the front door; snack dishes beside the couch in the den; hairbrush and clips on the kitchen counter. I'm a constant nag, and she's all over the place: haughty, arrogant, sulky, and mean. Grounding her for a week did nothing. Requiring her to clean the whole house only made her hostile, and we didn't speak to each other for several days. I recently came to the conclusion that she reacts angrily to her constant forgetfulness as a way to save face. She doesn't always fail to put things away; it's just often enough to drive me crazy, and she doesn't do it because she is bad. It is because she is still young with lots of changes happening at once. I considered what I had done when she was younger, and I now meet her at the front door, remind her where her sweater belongs, and at the end of the evening help her make sure that homework papers are in her pack for the next day. I find that we often chat about her day, her friends, and what's on her mind during these times together. She just can't do all that I was expecting her to do all the time on her own.*

*—Brenda, forty-four*

Sooner or later, all young teens will challenge their parents for more freedom. What they often do not understand is that with more freedom comes more responsibilities, and many are not up to the extra obligation. Being allowed to ride the bus downtown with friends on a Saturday morning carries the responsibility of telling parents where she is going and who she is going with, and of being back at the agreed-upon time. Implied is the expectation that she will be law-abiding and avoid shoplifting, vandalism, and other disruptive behavior. The privilege may also include the responsibility to refrain from accepting a ride from anyone and return home by bus. Explicitly made clear may be the necessity to call home if she needs help, misses the bus, or will be late for any reason. Being allowed to go to the movies with friends carries many of the same responsibilities. Stay at the movie theater; call when the movie is over; go next door to the pizza place; and stay put until picked up. Each family will have its own particular privilege or version of the rules. But, if the responsibilities of the freedom are not met, then we must lower our expectations, which includes limiting the freedom.

Please do not misunderstand us. We are not saying "Have no expectations." Children of all ages need to aspire to responsible, respectful, and loving behavior. And this will only happen if we expect this behavior—eventually. In our long-term vision of them, we hold them as productive and contributing members of our families, schools, and communities. Right now, however, between the ages of twelve and fifteen, **if they frequently fail to achieve what we expect of them, we must find the balance between challenging them to grow into more and more responsibility with the ability to succeed and function within the family without shame and guilt, or danger.** We do this by making sure that the tasks we set for them are not (because of their developmental stage) beyond their abilities to adequately perform *most of the time.*

*It took me two sessions of therapy to realize that I had failed my son by expecting too much of him at his age. I had totally forgotten my struggles with my own dad when I was fourteen. The fights my son and I had didn't compare to the ones I had with my dad about weeding the garden and chopping wood, until the day I got so mad at my son that I hit him. That was a pretty loud wake-up call that I wasn't handling things so well. The trouble started, big-time, when I offered my son a job at the store for twelve dollars an hour, if he took an Internet course on how to work the new software on my inventory program. He was very eager, astonished at the salary I offered, and thought that spending an hour a day on the five-week course would be simple. He was very motivated when he began until he really got into the material. After three days, his logging on became sporadic and stopped altogether within a week. It was then that I lost my temper, calling him lazy, stupid, and a failure. I thought I had made a very easy bargain with him, but my therapist helped me understand how much I could expect from my son at his age, and that I was expecting far too much. It took some time to repair the damage I had done, but as I gave my son tasks that took less time and were more manageable, supporting his efforts and periodically checking his progress, we regained the trust in each other that we had lost. I learned that I can't treat my family members like my employees, and that a family doesn't run like a business.*

*—Mike, father of Josh, fourteen*

## Use Immediate Accountability Loops

*Definition: accountable, adj.*

*1. Liable to being called to account; answerable; responsible.*

Like Mike's son in the previous story, teens in the falling years need close supervision and immediate feedback to keep them accountable for their responsibilities as family members. Waiting until the next day to approach a young teen about the dirty clothes left on the bathroom floor usually brings a dazed look of bewilderment to her eyes as she searches her memory to recall what we are talking about. Too many things have happened since then. The world has stopped several times while waiting for her boyfriend to call; she finally finished her term paper; the middle school Lions won their big game; and on and on. Picking up after herself was not high on her priority list. Her accountability loop must be short to avoid the arguments and rage that result from having issues left too long. A casual, "Oh, and make sure that your dirty clothes from the bathroom are in the hamper," before she goes to bed needs to be part of the regular nighttime routine. Consistency and kindness work much better than punishment or a big lecture about how sloppy she is the next morning. These interactions only lead to name-calling, stubbornness, and resentment on both sides. Like a lifeguard diligently watching the swimmers in a pool, parents of teens in the falling years must provide continuous and timely feedback. Hold them accountable with the simple direction to "Do it now," if the task has not been done.

When the stakes are higher, and our supervision and feedback must extend to the world beyond our family, we often need the help of other parents. The parents of our children's friends become important allies in keeping family rules and fences secure and strong. When daughter Sara is invited for a sleep-over at friend Janie's house, we call Janie's mother for a chat. Questions like, "How many friends is Janie having over?" and "Will you be home all weekend?" and "What are your rules about alcohol and pot?" are never out of line. If the answers from Janie's mother are not compatible with our family rules, then we have choices to make. We may decide on the spot that Sara may not go to Janie's for the sleep-over. Or, we may question Janie's mother further; tell her our concern; and come to an agreement. **Accountability loops work effectively when parents support parents.** A call back to Janie's mom to see how they all fared after the sleep-over is not only courteous but keeps the accountability loop, independently of our teens, intact and functioning well.

> *My daughter really wanted to go to a friend's birthday sleep-over, but they were planning to watch several video movies that I thought were totally inappropriate for thirteen-year-olds to see. I know my daughter would have been upset by the violent content. After talking with this girl's parents about my concerns, they were shocked to discover how objectionable the videos really were. Other selections were made that were acceptable to all of us, and my daughter happily went to the party.*
>
> *—Maylee, thirty-nine*

The parents of teens at Acalanes High School in Lafayette, California, take accountability and feedback seriously. Any parent willing to be called about school affairs, student activities, or individual student difficulties agrees to an asterisk next to their name in the Student Directory.

This mark means any parent may call to confirm whether "everybody in the class is going," to ask for support for a particularly hard decision, to keep up-to-date on current fads and fashions, or to sustain accountability loops.

**Relationships with the parents of our teenagers' friends are as important as their peer relationships.** These parents may not be the kinds of people we tend to choose as friends, but we have a natural and crucial link through our children. As family therapist Mary Pipher, Ph.D., writes in her book, *The Shelter of Each Other*, about rebuilding families and community, "We yearn for the same things . . . . most people believe that children should have certain rights—to physical and psychological safety, good schools, drug-free environments and moral teachings . . . . We want government to be kind and good . . . . we share basic moral values such as the belief in honesty, respect and compassion."[3] Through our love and concern for our children, we unite with other parents to support each other in the often arduous, always interesting task of raising teenagers.

MISCONCEPTION #3: **The third most common misconception parents have about teenagers is that they mean what they say.**

"She said she was leaving, so I packed her bag." Do not forget that our teens in the falling years are driven by the feeling life. They react emotionally to every word, action, and event they experience. Many of their verbal responses to us are instinctive attempts to protect their vulnerable feelings, divert our attention from the immediate issues, or to make a connection. It may be tempting to believe that our teens behave the way they do and say the things they do because:

- they are bad people;

- they are out to get us;

- they enjoy making our lives miserable;

- they are stupid and immature;

- we did something wrong;

- they are gathering research to write a book.

In fact, the cause of teenage behavior is none of these. The teenager is on a spiritual search for self. Although some behavior is culturally driven, the experimentation, criticism, and questioning are inherent in such a search. A person cannot develop a unique self without examining the values and mores held by his or her parents.

"But why does she have to do it so dramatically?"

"Does he have to cloud every remark in such heavy sarcasm?"

"Could we at least have a conversation in a normal tone of voice without the hysterics?"

"She acts like I shouldn't exist or have my own opinions."

"He speaks so hatefully to us all."

"How did I become so stupid all of a sudden?"

## Listen for the Positive Intent

Even with the maturity of years on our side, we sometimes have difficulty saying what we mean and clearly articulating our needs to others. Our young teens, ruled by their emotions, often blurt out the exact opposite of what they intend or need to say. **When we listen for the meaning beneath their words, we open a sacred portal to their souls, inviting true communication and understanding.** Nothing breaks through the heat of a conflict like the words, "Tell me more." "Can I help?" "That sounds hard." "You look angry." Staying calm and sane during a burst of profanity or violent threats is not always easy to do. If we remember, however, that during the falling years our teens do not necessarily mean what they say, we are better able to avoid taking things so personally and succumbing to the entangling traps of losing our temper, harboring hurt feelings, name-calling, or physical violence. Are the following scenarios familiar?

"I told her that she could not go to the concert on Saturday night. She yelled, 'You never let me do anything that's fun!' and slammed the door."

"When I asked him to clean up his room, he sneered, 'You _____! Just leave me alone!'"

"'I hate you and I hate this house,' he declared as he stomped out the front door."

"When I said 'No' to the skin-tight miniskirt for school, my daughter screamed, 'You treat me just like a baby!'"

"'You are so stupid. You don't understand a thing about me or my friends!' she blurted out, shaking with anger."

If we used a dictionary definition for the words our teenagers use, we couldn't help but be hurt, indignant, and angry. If we look for the real meaning beneath their words, the positive intent, we more clearly understand their needs, frustrations, and fears.

"You never let me do anything that's fun," might be translated as, "You have so many rules that by the time I get to do something, it isn't fun anymore." Or, "Your fear for me is so overwhelming that it spoils my ability to have fun."

"You _____! Just leave me alone!" could mean, "I'm feeling smothered. Please give me some room to be myself." Or, "My room is my own domain. I need my privacy."

"I hate you and I hate this house," implies "I miss you. You're always so busy working." Or, "I feel like a stranger in my own home."

"You treat me just like a baby!" may plead, "Look at me. I'm growing up." Or, "I do still need your guidance, but please consider all the pressures I'm under."

"You are so stupid. You don't understand a thing about me or my friends!" could be interpreted as, "I feel ignored by you, somehow misunderstood." Or, "Please listen to MY thoughts, ideas, and feelings without judging, criticizing, and lecturing."

The positive intent does *not* excuse hurtful, disrespectful, malicious, or violent words and deeds. Being free to express one's opinions, needs, and feelings carries a responsibility to speak and act so that the family member can hear and receive the intended message. An important part of parenting is the reflecting back to our teens how they affect us and others with their words and actions.

> *My mother recently shared that when I was a teen-ager, she often retreated to her bedroom to cry after we had an interaction. How was I to know how I affected her when she just went away?*
>
> —*Pat, thirty-eight*

It is no easy task to withstand the often angry and belligerent teenage facade we experience during the falling years. If looks could kill . . . ! It is vital, however, that we not allow ourselves to be bullied or abused by our children. "Your words hurt and are hard for me to hear. Please try again," may have to be said consistently until our teen gathers control and gets to the real issue.

Listening for the positive intent from the beginning of any encounter changes our position from foe to ally. We too easily forget that we really are on the same side as our young teenagers. We both need and want the same things:

- love
- connection
- freedom
- safety
- understanding
- fun
- creative endeavor
- meaningful work.

We both have the same fears and shortcomings:

- needing to be right
- losing our tempers
- thinking we know more than we really do
- nursing hurt feelings
- holding grudges
- plotting revenge.

Listening for the positive intent gets us out of the trap of focusing on negative behaviors and failures. Whatever our teenagers' words and deeds, they are expressing a need, a thought, an opinion, or a plea for help and understanding. **No matter how misdirected we think they are, they deserve our efforts to hear their undeveloped thinking, their hearts' desires, their survival needs, and their souls' callings.** The statement, "I understand what you are saying," does not mean, "I agree with you," as many of us fear. As adult leaders we can hold our own opinions, values, and mores while acknowledging those of our young teens. Why is it so difficult to listen to her belief that most teachers are hypocrites or that street people deserve social services? The capitalistic system will not fail nor will vigilantes burn down our houses. Patiently pointing out, "Have you considered this side of it?" rather than saying, "Your view is too limited," "Your thinking is immature," or "Your ideas don't make any sense!" enhances a give-and-take communication and nurtures self-esteem in the teen just entering the thinking life. Supporting our fledgling's efforts to express her thoughts, whether we think they are misguided, incomplete, or just plain crazy, feeds her soul and enables her to limp into the next stage of teenage development.

## Recommended Reading

*Uncommon Sense for Parents with Teenagers*, by Michael Riera, Celestial Arts, Berkeley, CA, 1995. This practical book by an experienced school counselor covers all issues of adolescence.

*Raising Black Children*, by James Comer and Alvin Poussaint, Penguin Books, New York, 1992. The authors provide resources for every African-American family and teachers of all races about the issues facing every teen complicated by the negative messages of racism.

*All Grown Up and No Place to Go*, by David Elkind, Addison-Wesley, Reading, MA, 1998. Elkind offers insight about our society's impulse to push children to grow up too fast.

*Parent/Teen Breakthrough*, by Miva Kirshenbaum and Charles Foster, Penguin Books, New York, 1991. This book provides a practical description of how to develop a relationship with teens, rather than battling for control over teens.

*The Complete Idiot's Guide to Parenting a Teenager*, by Kate Kelly, Simon and Schuster, New York, 1996. Kelly writes a warm and friendly guide to the serious problems and issues of adolescence.

## ENDNOTES

1. Gregory Bodenhamer, *Back in Control* (New York: Simon and Schuster, 1983), xii.

2. George Gerbner, "Stories That Hurt: Tobacco, Alcohol, and Other Drugs in the Mass Media," *Youth and Drugs: Society's Mixed Messages* (Rockville, MD: Office for Substance Abuse Prevention, 1990).

3. Mary Pipher, *The Shelter of Each Other: Rebuilding Our Families* (New York: Ballantine Books, 1996), 264-265.

# Part III:

## The Landing Years—From Fifteen to Seventeen

*"Well!" thought Alice to herself.*
*"After such a fall as this, I shall think nothing of*
*tumbling down-stairs! How brave they'll all*
*think me at home! Why, I wouldn't say anything*
*about it, even if I fell off the top of the house!"*
*(Which was very likely true.)*

—Lewis Carroll, *Alice's Adventures in Wonderland*

The next two years in a teenager's life serve as a transition between falling to earth and learning to live in his body and self. The landing years involve picking himself up, dusting himself off, and *beginning* to find a balance between his internal drama and his external life. Like recovering "land legs" after a long sea journey, a teen in the landing years *begins* to gain new balance and steadiness in his sense of responsibility, depth of thinking, and consistency of follow-through. His developing body causes him fewer surprises and less embarrassment. He experiences a new confidence in peer relationships. Most teens eventually settle into the routine of classes and study, discovering the subjects that captivate their imaginations and challenge their skills.

The weed we struggled to nurture during the falling years is less inward-turning, and *begins* to show more interest in how conditions in the world came to be the way they are; why we are his particular parents and family; and curious about how historical figures in the past influence who we are today. The spiritual search for self becomes less focused on the dark, inner depths, and our teen *begins* to look outwardly to the experiences and ideas of others. Although zealous in his beliefs, he is slower to judge until he has more facts; forgives more easily; and delights in the power of new knowledge and the authority of vocabulary.

> *At thirteen and fourteen, every action, look, and sentence my daughter made screamed, "Noooooooooo!"*

*Her whole demeanor oozed, "Noooooooooo!" It was "No!" to household chores; "No!" to family activities; "No!" to suggestions about her looks; "No!" to school classes and good grades; "No!" to family rules; "No!" to almost everything we held sacred or worthy of attention. Now, at sixteen-and-a-half, she is becoming more positive, more open to actually being alive. It seems that she had to say "No!" to everything before she could say "Yes!" to anything, living life, even.*

*—Rebecca, forty-three*

Parents and educators of sophomores and juniors would do well to welcome these middle teens to earth by supporting the deep sensitivity and deep sense of responsibility that is now beginning to develop within them. The problems of the world weigh heavily on their shoulders at this age, and the emergence of the Renaissance from the darkness of the Middle Ages offers a picture of what is beginning to happen in the inner life of our teenagers.

*Alice opened the door and found that it led into a small passage, not much larger than a rathole; she knelt down and looked along the passage into the loveliest garden you ever saw. How she longed to get out of that dark hall, and wander about among those beds of bright flowers and those cool fountains, but she could not even get her head through the doorway . . . . "I think I could, if only I knew how to begin." For, you see, so*

*many out-of-the-way things had happened lately, that
Alice had begun to think that very few things indeed
were really impossible.*

—Lewis Carroll, *Alice's Adventures in Wonderland* [1]

## ENDNOTES

1. Carroll, *Alice*, 8-9.

## ❧ CHAPTER FIVE ❧

# Willing, Feeling, and Thinking— The Landing Years

*Joy and grief are never far apart. In the same
street the shutters of one house are closed while
the curtains of the next are brushed by the
shadows of the dance. A wedding party returns
from the church; and a funeral winds to its door.
The smiles and sadness of life are the tragi-
comedy of Shakespeare. Gladness and sighs
brighten the dim mirror he beholds.*

—Robert Eldridge Willmott

## WILL AND BODY

By the ages of sixteen and seventeen our teens become taller than we are. The rapid changes they experienced during the landing years are slowing down, and they feel more at home in their bodies. No longer an enemy, the body becomes a source of pleasure to the teen in the middle years, stronger, more coordinated, and more reliable.

"I always tested my dad's strength against my own, even when I was a puny seven-year-old. Now he really has to push hard to get the best of me."

"Thank goodness I'm past the worst years of my face breaking out. I don't get so panicked about every little zit now."

"Giving a speech in front of class is not as bad as it was in ninth grade. Getting a 'hard on' is not as embarrassing to me now."

"I was really worried when I started to gain weight at thirteen. All my friends did too, but I thought I'd just keep on getting fatter. Last year I grew a lot taller, though, so it balanced itself out."

An inner sense of invincibility and immortality propels teens in the landing years to even greater risk-taking and more dangerous exploits than we knew about in the falling years. This risky experimentation, however, is motivated not by the insecurities we saw in the younger teen, but rather by the older adolescent's desire to savor life to its fullest. With new confidence, teens between fifteen and seventeen try to break through the boundaries of time and energy by participating in as many activities as interest them. Individual and team sports are high on the list of commitments, as well as musical lessons and ensembles, drama productions, choir groups, student government, club memberships, and part-time jobs, not to mention elaborate social activities with friends. If there is any time for sleeping and eating, all the better. The common draw-backs to all of this enthusiasm are that the middle teen may neither eat well nor get enough sleep. Their strong wills and new-found intellects carry them along until they fall ill.

> *I belonged to every club in my high school and was an officer in many of them. Play practices lasted far into the night; I helped run several campaigns for positions on Student Council; I competed in horseback riding events every weekend. That's only half of what I did. I could function for weeks on little sleep and then all of a sudden I'd land sick in bed for several days. All I would do was sleep. I was mad.*
>
> —*Jenny, thirty*

Other hazards in this quest for life lurk in the stress of over-committing oneself and failing to follow through. Overly zealous expectations take a toll on the self-esteem of our supposedly indomitable middle teens. Some just cannot manage to say "No" to anything for fear they'll miss something, although they fail to finish projects, over-shoot deadlines, and disappoint parents, teachers, friends, fellow officers, and teammates. They may also take dangerous risks, because they are not yet skilled in the art of looking at the consequences that come with experiencing all of life up close. Modern day versions of "chicken" and "Russian roulette" are still played out on the freeways, not to mention the risks taken in the dark at parties or the back seat of a parked car. A 1998 survey of over 16,000 American high school students by the Youth Risk Behavior Surveillance Research Section asked teens about their activities during a thirty-day period. According to Laura Kann, chief of the project, answers indicated that "too many kids practice behaviors that place them at risk for unnecessary mortality and morbidity." [1]

For example:

- Fifty percent had at least one alcoholic drink, and 33 percent had five or more.

- Seventeen percent drove after drinking, and 36 percent had been driven by a person who had been drinking.

- Thirty-six percent smoked at least one cigarette, and 16 percent smoked on at least twenty out of the thirty days. Seventy percent tried cigarettes during that month.

- Eighteen percent said they had carried a weapon such as a gun, knife, or club.

- Nineteen percent admitted rarely or never wearing a seat belt.

- One in five students reported that they had seriously considered suicide during the past year, and 15 percent had actually developed a specific plan.

- Forty-eight percent of all students said they had had sex; 16 percent said they had had four or more partners; and 7 percent had lost their virginity by age thirteen. About 43 percent of sexually active teens reported not using a condom the last time they had sex. [2]

In the middle years, an adolescent's sexual desires, feeling life, fledgling thinking life, and cultural pressures collide to create potentially lethal choices and actions, as the previous statistics indicate.

## THE FEELING LIFE

During the early teen years (thirteen to fifteen), we saw the life of desires—the soul—come into full bloom. Acting on the impulse of sexual desire, young teens were susceptible to risky sexual encounters absent of thought, choice, and consideration of the consequences. Every decision and observation was made from the heart and critical or analytical thinking was secondary.

"This is a great school. The teachers are nice here."

"My little brother is stupid. He gets in my way all the time."

"No matter what's at stake, human life must be preserved."

"Why can't my parents just leave me alone? I'm old enough to go out with a senior!"

These statements reflect how desires and opinions are intricately linked with the teenager, herself. She is her desires. A gradual shift from the complete immersion in feelings, beginning between the fifteenth and sixteenth years, allows new perspective of self and others to form. The grip of desires begins to give way to analytical thinking. During the later landing years (sixteen through seventeen), teenagers begin to step back, to separate self from their longings, to observe, "I have desires, and I can make choices about them." The developing intellect begins to interact with feelings to form opinions now once-removed from pure passionate impulses.

"I think this is a good school, because most graduates go on to college."

"My little brother is a pest sometimes, but he needs someone like me to show him around life."

"Humans deserve to die with dignity."

"My parents still don't understand much, but that older guy and I didn't have a lot to talk about."

Without parental supervision and structured activities, the chances of a sexual encounter remain high during the middle years. Direct communication and accurate information from parents are paramount to prevent the early sexual anguish of unplanned pregnancies, sexually transmitted diseases, and violent or frightening experiences. Many of us probably remember THE BIG TALK from Mom or Dad, awkwardly explaining "the birds and the bees," or the embarrassment of coming out of the gym after having seen THE FILM in sixth grade. Although we may have walked away from these initiations more confused than ever—or thoroughly disgusted—they were important (however imperfect) means of getting accurate information. Be careful not to assume that our young teens know it all, because much of their "knowledge" comes from either the unreliable, anecdotal evidence of peers, or the equally unreliable fantasy world of movies and television. We must not leave our teenager's sex education to the media. Many of the facts are distorted, and sexual content is heavily overlaid with violence, sexism, competition, or sophomoric humor. The portrayal of a respectful and loving sexual relationship is exceedingly rare. What our teens see are sexual *encounters* with little genuine intimacy, constancy, commitment, communication, or safety. If teenagers accept the media's message—that sex is the goal, the prize, the pot of gold at the end of the rainbow (which is what their hormones are telling them)—they will develop a skewed picture of the part that sex plays in a long-term, intimate relationship. To them, in their perpetually aroused state, sex is the relationship. Parents must teach their teens that a relationship is much more than having sex: being able to be themselves when they are with the other person; feeling listened to and understood; having fun; laughing together; safely sharing deep, intimate feelings; learning new ideas and attitudes; and feeling safe. When children learn that love grows from respecting another person's likes, dislikes, thoughts, and needs, they develop a perspective that allows sex to have its appropriate place within a relationship as one of many ways to give and receive love with our mates.

The best way for our children to learn about sex is by experiencing an affectionate, caring, and respectful relationship between two adults—parents, partners, grandparents, caregivers, or other role models. In the course of daily living, optimum moments arise to talk with our teens about giving and receiving love, showing honor and respect for one another, and to answer their intimate questions about sex. Any little opening will do. A silence while mother and daughter fold laundry; while mother and son do dishes; while father and daughter ride to the grocery store; while father and son cook dinner. Parenting advisors Linda and Richard Eyre, authors of *Teaching Your Children Values*, suggest that parents and their teens actually rehearse what to do in the situations that they are likely to find themselves in. A more mature version of a game for younger children, called "What If," can be extremely insightful and helpful. For example: "What if you are at a movie and your boyfriend puts his arm around you?" "What if he starts kissing your neck?" "What if he touches your breast?" "What if you get a hard-on?" "What if your girlfriend wants to go home?" "What if you are at a party, all the lights are out, and your friends are all making out?"

We applaud the current trend of hanging out in groups of friends, rather than the single-couple dating that was so popular during the 1950s and 1960s. There is often protection in a group where teens are less inclined to go "too far" sexually, and individuals tend to focus more on group dynamics and activities. Although group mentality can degenerate into mob mentality, and teens can feel pressured to do drugs, smoke, drink, or have sex, close friends often stick together to manage such pressures. By redefining dating to mean, "going out with a group of friends," we provide a safety net for our teens against the pressures of premature involvement in risky activities. Many parents delay their young teens from dating alone until they are sixteen, but most sixteen-year-olds are not yet ready for this challenge, and many are secretly relieved to delay this event. We suggest that the privileges of dating alone wait until after high school graduation. This is an obvious rite-of-passage for entering a more mature phase of life and should not be rushed, although it's hard to convince most teens that it's well worth the wait.

## Ideal Love and Sexual Love

A crush in the falling years is a version of ideal love made famous by the troubadours of Medieval Europe. This is worship from afar and inspires the lover to expansive thoughts and glorious deeds beyond his usual capabilities and inclinations. He is in love with the entire world, with all of humanity. Like the unconditional love of a very small child, the object of the teenage crush is revered as a golden symbol of perfection. Fifteenth-century poet and mystic, Kabir, wrote of his ideal love for God.

> *My body and my mind are in depression because you*
> *are not with me.*
> *How much I love you and want you in my house!....*
> *I don't really care about food, I don't really care about sleep,*
> *I am restless indoors and outdoors....*
> *How restless Kabir is all the time!*
> *How much he wants to see the Guest!* [3]
>
> —Kabir, *The Kabir Book*

As sexual desire develops during the middle teens, a danger arises. Ideal love, expansive and generous, is transmuted into sexual love, possessive and confining. Sexual love is an important part of loving but not the answer to our dreams that the modern media would have us believe. For the teenager, sexual love is often an assist in the striving for independence from authority, in the development into an individual self. A couple sees themselves as two against the world and loses themselves in the need to rebel by sneaking out late at night to meet or by becoming sexually involved.[4] Kabir says:

> . . . *The truth is you turned away yourself,*
> *and decided to go into the dark alone.*
> *Now you are tangled up in others, and have forgotten*
> *what you once knew,*
> *and that's why everything you do has some weird*
> *failure in it.*[5]

—Kabir, *The Kabir Book*

The biggest challenge for teen couples in the landing years is to understand that sexual love comes from the desires of the body. A whole loving involves the heart and mind, as well as the body, and includes a love and recognition of the other's higher, spiritual self. This love creates such joy that the lovers want to bring it as a balm to the entire world; to ease the pain of poverty, prejudice, ignorance, illness, and despair.

The passion and longing of teenage desire may bring up painful memories and tremendous fear for parents. Our first instinct is to forbid the relationship, usually creating resentment and anger, if not open rebellion. To err in the other direction by pushing our teens into exclusive, intimate relationships is just as counterproductive. Our challenge is to find the balance between supporting our teen's love relationships while setting the rules for appropriate behavior.

So, what do we do when we find a diaphragm, condoms, or birth control pills among our son's or daughter's things? This discovery provides the perfect opportunity for that discussion about sex, friendship, love, and intimacy that we may have been putting off. During a quiet moment, calmly admit to your teen that you found a diaphragm, for example, in her dresser drawer and ask her to tell you about it. If she is hesitant, questions such as "Where did you get it?" and "Why?" are appropriate. She will probably try to divert the attention from the diaphragm to the act of your snooping in her room. Although this may be a pertinent issue, it is one to be explored at another time. For now, direct her back to the diaphragm by saying, "I may have snooped, but now, tell me about the diaphragm." Listen carefully. It may be that on a whim she and a friend went to a birth control clinic to get protection, just in case. It may be that she and her boyfriend went a little further than she was prepared for. She got scared. She decided to be ready next time. Or, she possibly feels pushed by her boyfriend to get more physically involved than she really wants to, and your discovery and queries are just the lifeline that she was hoping for. Whatever the case, tell her about love and friendship and intimacy. Then tell her about sex and the responsibilities that go along with it. Tell her that her body belongs to her, and until she is old enough to assume the responsibility for it, you will help her abide by the rule that she refrain from sex until she is at least eighteen. The truth is that no young couple can feel perfectly safe and comfortable about being sexually involved. Unless they go to a motel—and few have the chutzpah to do that—they are few places for sexual intimacy that don't carry the fear of discovery besides the discomfort of a car seat.

Talk with your teen about both sides of the issue—developing passion *and* the feelings of not being ready. Support her feelings of uncertainty and her right to say "No," whatever situation she finds herself in. It may be possible to redirect her teenage passion by providing opportunities or encouraging activities that require creative and active participation, such as theater, political activism, and creative writing. Introduce her to the love poems of the Brownings, Shakespeare, and Kabir.

If you have found condoms in your son's drawer, give him the same information. Restate the family rule. Tell him about the number-one rule of sexual intimacy: The words "No," "Stop," and "I don't want to," mean "No," "Stop," and "I don't want to." Tell him to never use his penis to hurt anyone, including himself. That means never doing anything that he is uncomfortable about, thinks is wrong, or doesn't want to, no matter what society or his friends say is cool.

For some reason, many parents have accepted the idea that casual sex among our teenagers is their prerogative. We disagree. Expressing our sexuality with someone we care for is another privilege that comes with the rights and responsibilities of being an adult. Consider the astounding rates of teenage pregnancy and abortion, the high occurrence of sexually transmitted diseases, and the potentially deadly risk of AIDS.[6] These statistics do not support arguments in favor of teenage sexual experimentation and involvement. The emotional scars left from an abortion or from giving up a baby for adoption last a lifetime, no matter how old the mother. Early sexual experiences leave physical—as well as emotional—scars if the encounter was pressured, coerced, or violent. For some teens, the guilt they carry about their sexual feelings and actions is enough to affect their healthy sexual development.

It is possible to offer empathy toward and understanding of our teen's feelings, while at the same time firmly holding to the family rule that sexual involvement be avoided until they are eighteen or older, and that dating is done in groups. "You may not believe me, but I was in love with my chemistry lab partner. I focused so much on her, I didn't get much out of lab," reveals Dad to his teenage son. "I know you would like to date alone, but group dating is the rule. Why not ask her over for dinner on Friday night?" The most important point of all this is to acknowledge that sexual feelings and the impulse toward sexual experimentation are natural teenage experiences and are acceptable to have and to talk about. Some parents find the discussion is easier within the context of a class given for teens and their parents by organizations such as Planned Parenthood or local health clinics or hospitals. Amidst the facts, however, remember how important are the values of friendship, love, and intimacy.

*The flute of interior time is played whether we hear it or not,*
*What we mean by "love" is its sound coming in.*
*When love hits the farthest edge of excess,*
*it reaches a wisdom.*
*And the fragrance of that knowledge!*
*It penetrates our thick bodies,*
*it goes through walls—*
*Its network of notes has a structure as if a million suns were arranged inside.*
*This tune has truth in it.*
*Where else have you heard a sound like this?* [7]

Kabir, *The Kabir Book*

## The Spiritual Quest in the Landing Years

Teens in the falling years experience a spiritual longing for a home; a home where they are accepted for who they are, how they feel, and what they think. What they experience instead is alienation, misunderstanding, and loneliness.

During the early landing years (fifteen to sixteen), teens reach a turning point, a fork in the path that requires a choice between saying "Yes" or "No" to life. They require something meaningful to latch onto now, something that ignites their imaginations and fires their creativity. Churches put more emphasis on their youth programs for teens in this age group, because they are hungry for structure, deep contemplation, open dialogue, and charitable service. Teens in the landing years are an enormous, untapped resource of willing volunteers.

Teenagers, now easily influenced by philosophies that appeal to their spiritual longings, may adopt unconventional religious beliefs. What if a teen's spiritual path conflicts with her parents' views? We have all read about the cults that brainwash their devotees, cutting them off from the outside world, and we do not want our children to be controlled or hurt. The best way to deal with our teen's spiritual search is to avoid criticism about her ideas, lest we push her further into something that she was merely investigating. Be open and interested in what her beliefs are, what appeals to her about a certain religious group or spiritual path, and why. What arouses fear in us may be another, although different, way of worshiping the Divine. As the teen grows, these beliefs will either mature or transform into other ways that nourish the spirit and soothe the soul. If the adolescent beliefs are truly dangerous or frightening, then finding out everything about the creed and the group perpetuating it will help parents know where to find help. Seeking the counsel of a minister, priest, rabbi, shaman, or transpersonal therapist often offers the guidance and reassurance a parent needs when spiritual conflicts arise.

Waldorf high schools recognize this crucial turning point when teenagers begin to grapple with themselves and the choice between life and death. In the eleventh grade they recognize Shakespeare's Hamlet in themselves: Hamlet, who loses himself in the emotional life; Hamlet, whose father is displaced by another; Hamlet, whose mother marries again, too soon; Hamlet, who flirts with madness; Hamlet, who contemplates suicide. Each year Meg Gorman, Waldorf high-school teacher, asks her juniors to close their eyes and raise their hands if they have ever thought about committing suicide. She relates that twenty years ago, about five in a class of thirty raised their hands. Today, almost every hand in the class goes up. "I never tell them the answers at this age. There aren't any, anyway," she says. They come to terms with themselves and their own answers with Hamlet." [8]

## THE THINKING LIFE

At this stage of growth it is impossible to explore willing, feeling, and thinking as separate functions. Thinking is definitely emerging as the focus of development, and its effects on willing and feeling cannot be overlooked. The thinking life allows the teen in the landing years a new perspective on his own feelings and actions, as well as the feelings and actions of others. She is starting to be able to step back from the intensity of desires and feelings. "I am afraid" is evolving into "I feel afraid." The feelings are no less potent and real, but she is less caught in the pathos of them. He is more able to make reflective statements, such as "I *really* yelled at my brother so that my parents would forget that I hadn't done my homework." Rather than a blatant "Teachers should be eliminated," she is able to reflect, "Mean and inept teachers should be fired." More and more often, parents experience a slight shift in a heretofore immovable opinion: "I sort of see what you mean . . . ." Or "I see how that *could* be . . . ." Teens in the landing years are learning to embrace the world as they see it—the pain, ugliness, and deception that they wanted to previously deny. Now they yearn to understand it, to trace how things got to be this way. Ancient history, the stories of the Old Testament, and Homer bring fascinating perspectives. Questions such as, "Why are these my particular parents?" carry great import, and adopted children in the middle years wonder and ask questions about their biological parents and where they came from.[9]

The development of the thinking life allows teenagers to come out of the extremes of withdrawal or aggression that may have characterized the falling years. They begin to laugh more, to enjoy communicating with parents, to be better able to relate to teachers, and to be more tolerant of younger siblings.

*Until I was sixteen or seventeen, I wanted my little brother to drop off the face of the earth. As far as I was concerned, he had no use at all. He just got in my*

*way and made my life harder with all his questions,*
*silly comments, and weird ideas. Plus, he liked to fol-*
*low me around, and he spied on me and my friends.*
*Then, he sort of became all right, you know? I still*
*didn't like him much, but I could appreciate some of*
*his talents, like these neat cartoons he could draw. It*
*was strange. I don't know if he got better as he got*
*older, or if I did.*

—*James, twenty-one*

Middle teens are now beginning to realize that some laws must be accepted and obeyed. These are the years when teens customarily take training in driver's education and obtain their driver's licenses. The trouble is that teens are *just now beginning* to understand cause and effect, the reason for traffic laws, and the importance of safe driving habits. A look at the statistics makes us wonder whether we should reconsider putting such a powerful and dangerous machine as the automobile under the control of middle teens. Accidents in motor vehicles are by far the leading cause of death among teenagers ages thirteen to nineteen, and beginning drivers carry the greatest risk. Teen drivers are more often at fault when an accident occurs, and the majority of deaths involve teens as passengers with another teen driving. Sixteen-year-olds have by far the highest rate of passenger deaths than all other drivers.[10] It is not hard to realize that lack of driving experience and immaturity are the main reasons for such high casualty rates. When a dangerous situation arises, young drivers are less able to respond appropriately than the driver with more years behind the wheel. The following situations characterize teen accidents and cause the highest death rates:

- tailgating

- speeding

- thrill seeking and risk taking

- single vehicle accidents

- night driving (One-half of teenage deaths occur between 9 P.M. and 6 A.M.) [11]

- high occupancy

- driver error

- lack of seat belts

- underestimation of dangers

- inability to respond to dangerous situations [12]

Ironically, statistics show that high school Driver's Education courses do *not* improve teenagers' driving records. These training programs simply put too many young drivers on the road. [13] Many states are responding to the dangers that inexperienced drivers bring to the highways by increasing the age of licensure, enforcing early night-time curfews, and introducing graduated licensing procedures. These programs include an extended learner's permit whereby the young driver must be accompanied by an adult, is banned from using major roads, is allowed only a limited number of passengers, and faces high penalties for any violation of the rules. After the teenager accrues a certain number of driving hours without infractions, a restricted license is achieved. An unrestricted license is granted only after a teen turns eighteen or twenty-one and has a proven safe driving record. In other words, a teenager earns the right to drive through his performance and driving ability, not simply because he turns sixteen.

Parents can also provide driving restrictions that increase the safety of their teens. Driving curfews and other agreements, like the following, lower the odds on accidents.

## A Contract Between Parents and Teen Drivers [14]

It is understood that having a driver's license and driving a motor vehicle are privileges. Any privilege has to be earned, and it must be earned on a continual basis. This means that driving privileges may be revoked by either parent due to an infraction of the following rules:

1. Breaking the driving laws or abusing a motor vehicle can result in the loss of driving privileges, even if we learn about it from a source other than the police. You never know who may be observing you.

2. You will strive to maintain your grades, conduct, and attitude at the same high level as when we granted you driving privileges.

3. No one else should be allowed to drive a vehicle entrusted to you. This means that you may not lend your vehicle to friends.

4. If you are ever in a condition that might render you less than 100% competent behind the wheel of a car, phone us at home or wherever we are. This will not result in the loss of driving privileges.

5. You are never to be a passenger in a car in which the driver should not be driving. A call to come and get you will not result in the loss of driving privileges. If you cannot reach us, hire a taxi. We will pay for it and there will be no punishment.

_____          _____
Parents' Signature          Teen's Signature

◆ ◆ *Don* | As a therapist, I find kids easier to work with at this age. They see more easily that certain behaviors do more harm to *themselves* than to the others they want to affect. For example, one girl was so angry at her parents that she wanted to punish them. Her way was to stop eating. She had reason to be angry, and I asked her to think of how she could punish her parents without punishing herself as well, since her current behavior could result in serious illness. Her solution was ingenious. She choose to become a vegetarian, studied nutrition thoroughly, and continuously lectured her family about their unhealthy diets. She also took up weight-lifting and became skilled in Aikido. She not only succeeded in getting her overly strict parents off her back, she glowed with good health.

It is with deep understanding of the needs of adolescents that the Waldorf high school curriculum includes learning the art of stringing a loom and weaving during the tenth-grade year. Teens at this age are beginning to see that the fabric of the Universe is precise; that if one thread is dropped, the entire creation is altered. From the new perspective of analytical thinking, they learn to see how the process of life works, step by intricate step.

## Recommended Reading

*A Parent's Guide for Suicidal and Depressed Teens*, by Kate Williams, Hazelden, Center City, MN, 1995. This personal account by a parent of a depressed teen offers hope as well as practical advice.

*Helping Your Depressed Teenager*, by Gerald Oster and Sarah Montgomery, John Wiley and Sons, New York, 1995. The authors offer good examples of teens in trouble and an excellent guide to medications effective in treating depression.

*Changing Roles, Changing Bodies*, by Ruth Bell and other co-authors of *Our Bodies, Ourselves* together with members of the Teen Book Project, 3rd. ed., Random House, New York, 1998. This is a detailed and insightful guide for all issues concerning teens.

*Smart Sex: 501 Reasons to Hold off On Sex*, by Susan Browning, Fairview Press, Pogany, Minneapolis, 1998. The author candidly gives information about sex, feelings of rejection and wanting to impress peers, other ways to make love, and the dangers of teenage sexual activity.

*The First Time*, by Karen Bouris, Conari Press, Berkeley, CA, 1993. This is a book for both teens and their parents with insight from 150 women and their sexual stories.

*Surviving Teen Pregnancy*, rev., by Shirley Arthur, Morning Glory Press, Buena Park, CA, 1996. When an unplanned pregnancy occurs, this book can provide a guide to the important issues.

*Teenage Roadhogs*, by Michael Schein, Macmillan, New York, 1997. Written for parents and teens, this book is a common-sense and humorous guide for young drivers.

*Raising a Thoughtful Teenager*, by Ben Kamin, Penguin Books, New York, 1996. Rabbi Ben Kamin raises important insights about helping our teens understand the problems of the world.

*The Moral Intelligence of Teenagers*, by Robert Coles, Penguin Books, New York, 1997. This sensitive book shows parents how to teach children to be kind and supportive, and to respect themselves and those around them.

*Chicken Soup for the Teenage Soul*, by Jack Canfield, Mark Hansen, and Kimberly Kirberger, Health Communications, Inc., Deerfield Beach, FL, 1997. These stories full of struggle and success will inspire any teen.

*Chicken Soup for the Teenage Soul II* and *Chicken Soup for the Teenage Soul Journal*, Jack Canfield, Mark Hansen, and Kimberly Kirberger, Health Communications Inc., Deerfield Beach, FL, 1998. More of the same, plus a unique place for teens to record their own private thoughts and personal stories.

## ENDNOTES

1. Cox News Service, "Teen Survey Finds High-Risk Activities," *San Francisco Chronicle*, Friday, 14 Aug. 1998, sec. A8.

2. Ibid.

3. Robert Bly, trans., *The Kabir Book* (Boston: Beacon Press, 1977), 20.

4. Staley, *Between Form*, 184-185.

5. Bly, *Kabir*, 23.

6. Beverly Engel, *Beyond the Birds and the Bees* (New York: Pocket, 1997).

7. Bly, *Kabir*, 21.

8. Gorman, lecture.

9. Although it is hard to predict how adopted children will fare when they reach adolescence, many adopted teens experience identity confusion, difficulty with new freedoms, and issues about belonging. If adopted teens feel reluctant to go to school and they lose interest in their studies, an experienced professional can help families provide the support needed for exploring the teens' feelings about being adopted. The following resouces are also helpful: The National Adoption Information Clearinhouse website, http://www.calib.com/naic/publications/adolesce.htm; The Post Adoption Center for Education and Research website, http://www.no.com/pacer/; You're Our Child: The Adoption Experience, by Jerome Smith and Franklin Miroff; and Searching for a Past, by Jayne Schooler.

10. Insurance Institute for Highway Safety, 1998 report, "Speed Kills," *The Washington Post*, 23 Feb. 1999, sec.WH5.

11. "Facts 1996 Fatalities: Teenagers," Insurance Institute for Highway Safety Page, n.d., http://www.hwysafety. org/facts/teens. htm, 11 Dec.1997.

12. Ibid.

13. Ibid.

14. Website: http://nbcin.wnyt.com/contract.html, WYNT TV, Albany, NY.

# CHAPTER SIX

# Fences for the Landing Years

*This time, like all times, is a very good one,*
*if we but know what to do with it.*

—Ralph Waldo Emerson

O ur middle teens still need parental supervision, fences (limits and boundaries), and follow-through. But unlike teens in the falling years, middle teens have skills of analytical, cause-and-effect, and logical thinking that permit more movement, more privacy, and more independence. We are not saying that a complete metamorphosis has occurred. Middle teens still behave in ways that make our hair turn gray. They still have lapses in common sense and swish, swish, pause thinking patterns. Some teens get into real trouble during the landing years, for various reasons. Remember that all children develop in their own natural ways and at their own natural paces, and our age divisions are based on how human children would develop left unhindered by the influences of biology, culture, and family nurture. Some teens are "late-bloomers" and continue to fall way past the landing of many of their peers. Deep depression, learning disabilities, and other problems caused by chemical imbalances may keep teens from entering the transition years on the "schedule" we present here. In addition to continuous and consistent parental supervision, involvement, and firm family rules, parents may find family counseling necessary to help them and their teens through the rough and ragged times.

The challenge for teens sixteen through seventeen is to negotiate a balance between the pull of the outside world with the needs of the inner self. Betty Staley, Waldorf educator and author of *Between Form and Freedom: A Practical Guide to the Teenage Years*, describes a tension experienced by all human beings—the tension between the physical and the spiritual worlds. She writes, ". . . we feel at times pulled in two directions. Where the worlds of body and spirit meet, they create the realm of the human soul . . . .the soul-life is always in flux . . . the crossing point between inner and outer realities. Adolescents live right in the middle of this tension, unable to find a secure place in the center. Their needs and desires swirl and storm within them—and sometimes sweep them away." [1] Middle teens are often at the mercy of the forces of the outer world—the desire to belong, to make change, to be actively engaged, and to know the facts—that appear to conflict with the needs of the inner self—the need to be apart, to look inward, to be still, and to create from the imagination. They must learn to reconcile the tension between the two worlds of body and spirit by trusting the feeling life, the mediator between willing and thinking. [2] If the Will succumbs to the allure of the outside world, a teen finds himself lost in too much intensity and activity, separated from his inner needs and desires. Conversely, a teen too intro-spective and focused on the inner life becomes reclusive, self-indulgent, and depressed. Of course, most of us tend to be one or the other, but the biggest challenge for parents during the landing years is to help teens achieve a balance that includes being healthy, safe, and actively engaged as creative members of the family and the community.

## KEEPING TEENS HEALTHY

*I live in that solitude which is painful in youth,*
*but delicious in the years of maturity.*

—Albert Einstein

When our children were infants and toddlers, they thrived on a regular rhythm of activity and rest, solitude and togetherness. In fact, all humans flourish when these states of being are balanced. The middle adolescent, however, is apt to get caught in one or the other, needing parental guidance to find a healthy symmetry during the landing years. Where one teen becomes reclusive, pensively holed up in her room for hours, another is forever on the phone, filling his calendar with study dates, ball games, movie nights, and sleep-overs, a constant flow of friends between the refrigerator and the family room. Both are doing what comes naturally, but too much of only one way of being makes Jane or Joe a dull girl or boy. Too much community or too much solitude leads to imbalance, which can lead to illness. We do not mean to confuse *balance* with *equal*; it would be impossible to give an equal number of hours to being with friends and spending time alone. Our teens need help finding what is commonly called an "optimal balance," enough time alone and enough time with friends to nurture this particular teen's soul. Although we may think they are the same thing, rest, solitude, and silence are three different needs in the lives of our middle teens. Rest balanced with physical activity, solitude with community, and silence with sound allows our teenagers to navigate the tension between their inner and outer worlds.

> *I've had to struggle to make friends—girlfriends are impossible—and I only have two best friends. I read about these guys who become hackers and computer nerds. Sometimes I think that I should do that, and just spend all my time in cyberspace.*
>
> —Dean, sixteen

## Rest and Physical Activity

It is easy to see that teens need adequate sleep and not that easy to provide it. They have the energy of youth on their side, and with their insatiable eagerness to experience all of life, many get by—for a time—on continuous late nights and early mornings. Of course, there are also the teens who seem to sleep all of the time, never able to catch up or to get enough. Most humans need eight to nine hours of sleep, and a recent study indicates that most Americans are sleep-deprived, just getting by on five to seven.[3] A tired populace has great impact on the incidence of job and school absenteeism, auto accidents, work injuries, poor career and school performance, rash judgments, hasty decision-making, strained family dinners, and violence.

A reasonable curfew during the week and on weekends helps foster the habit of getting enough sleep. We cannot force our teens to sleep, but being home at a sensible hour on weeknights with television, telephone, and music off-limits after 10 P.M. encourages them to study, read for pleasure, or rest. "But, I'm resting when I watch TV or listen to music," they protest, and this may seem to be the case, but these activities do not have the restorative powers of sufficient hours of sleep.

🕸 🕸 *DON* | Here is a typical family counseling session with Mom, Dad, and sixteen-year-old son. Son has a history of breaking his curfew and has just been picked up and brought home by the police for wandering the streets with friends at 3 A.M., although no charges were filed. The mother tearfully says, "I don't want him to think that we don't trust him." I say to her, "No, you don't want him to think that you don't *love* him. You *don't* trust him, because of his track record with keeping curfew. Love is freely given. Trust is earned, and your son has not earned your trust. If you don't set a reasonable standard of behavior for him, you rob your son of his chance to feel good about himself, to prove himself. When he does that, he earns a later curfew without feeling guilty and bad."

"But how do we set a reasonable curfew and hold our teenagers to it?" we wonder. Consider these points:

- What are the needs of the family concerning the evening rhythm?

- How will the time our teens come home affect other family members?

- Are there younger ones with an early bedtime?

- How much sleep does our teen need to keep that optimal balance we spoke of earlier?

- What are the parents' needs for sleep, and do we really rest while our children are out?

It may be difficult to swallow, but a teen is a family member and has a responsibility for helping make the family work. A curfew may be set according to family needs.

- Talk with teachers and other parents of middle teens. What curfew do they set for their children during the week?

- On weekends? This information wards off the common argument, "But, so-and-so doesn't have to come home until 2 A.M.!"

- Be conservative when setting curfews. It is much easier—and gratifying to a teen—to extend a curfew than it is to set one back.

- Acknowledge a teen for keeping curfew. Nothing works like encouragement and success.

- If sneaking out after bedtime is a problem, sit down together for a serious conversation. This chat lets a teen know that, contrary to what he may believe, his parents do "have a clue" about what he is doing.

- Explain the seriousness of his actions. Tragedies have happened when a teenager was mistaken for an intruder climbing in or out of a bedroom window by an armed family member or the police.

- Outline the proper way to be late:
  a) A teen must always call to let her parents know where she is, why she is late, and when she will be home.
  b) She must ring the doorbell to be let in and to announce that she is home.
  c) Let the teen know that unless the rules of curfew are followed, the locks will be changed.

- When a teen consistently breaks curfew, he loses the privilege of going out at all. These evenings at home provide space for parents to spend more time with busy teens; to discover the reasons for being chronically late; and to emphasize that curfews are for safety, not for punishment.

We really do want them to have fun, but combined with the right to go out is the responsibility to follow family rules.

As a counterpoint to sleep, physical activity tones and strengthens the body, reduces the effects of stress, and ensures peaceful rest. The release of endorphins—the body's natural "feel good" hormones—during strenuous physical activity acts as a powerful countermeasure, or even a prevention, for the depression that so often plagues adolescents. Organized team sports through high schools and city recreation departments develop cooperation, teach fundamentals (paramount to avoiding injury), and promote a sense of membership and belonging. Individual sports, such as in-line skating, bicycling, and horseback riding, offer challenge and mastery. Pick-up games in the park or neighborhood provide spontaneity and fun for all ages. Even a physically reluctant teen can be encouraged to walk the dog, bike to the store, or hike in a natural setting with family or friends. Whatever it is, regular physical activity is an antidote for the erratic emotional ups and downs that often accompany adolescence.

## Body Image and Eating Disorders

Both girls and boys face the painful issues of belonging. They want to be part of a group, to fit in, to be just like everyone else. They crave a unique anonymity, being known for themselves, while at the same time not standing out too much from the group. This need to be noticed, yet not noticed, challenges self-esteem—usually the part of self-esteem that is intertwined with appearance. "I love this blouse, but I can't wear it with that skirt!" "I like my hair short, because it stays out of my eyes when I play basketball, but all the guys are wearing their hair long in front." The importance of how one looks begins, for most of us, at birth, and few of us escape this cultural obsession. Billboards, magazine articles and advertisements, television shows and commercials, popular music, movies, and even computer programs tell and show us how we must look to be cool, loved, and successful. The tragedy of having to look a certain way to belong is that fashion is fickle and narrow-minded. Few of us ever fit the current look. The minute we have our curly hair straightened, curls are back in. Women have breast implants, and the Twiggy look comes round again. Men invest in colorful shirts, and gray becomes the color hit of the season. We attain the streamlined body of the swimmer, and then the muscular build of the weight lifter creates waves.

Because belonging is so important to teenagers, they are especially vulnerable to the whims of our appearance-driven society. Although girls seem to be more at risk, boys as well sometimes go to physical extremes to be popular. For many teenagers, the body becomes a battleground. This culture's worship of thinness drives girls, especially, to count calories, to deny themselves certain foods, to diet, and to overexercise, some beginning as early as fifth grade.[4] This behavior intensifies as girls begin the *natural*, normal weight gain in preparation for the onset of menstruation. Both boys and girls who participate in sports, such as wrestling, gymnastics, ballet, swimming, and track, face the pressures of meeting the weight limitations in the process of normal physical development.

Fewer boys develop eating disorders, and the causes may be somewhat different from girls. Where the motivation for girls involves weight, boys are more often concerned with shape and muscle definition, improving athletic performance, or slimming to please a homosexual lover. About 21 percent of males with eating disorders are gay.[5] Eating disorders in teen males are not diagnosed as readily as in females for various sociocultural reasons:

- Boys experience less pressure to be slim;

- Doctors are less likely to consider the diagnosis;

- Family and friends are less apt to recognize it;

- Symptoms are less obvious than the common loss of menstrual periods for girls;

- Males are more hesitant to seek help because of the social stigma of having a female or gay problem.[6]

*I was what lots of people call a "chubby" kid. I just grew that way. My mom fretted about my weight, urging me to eat fruits and veggies and to avoid all the snacks that kids love. Well, that was okay, but she also forced me into all sorts of physical activities—gymnastics, swimming, and volleyball—hoping that exercise would help slim me down. I'm thankful for the friends I made and the fun I had, but the pressure to compete—and to be thin—became overwhelming. I'm not a thin person; I never will be, but you can't tell my mom that. In high school, she was so worried that I wouldn't have a boyfriend because of my weight. Don't get the wrong impression. I was not fat. I was five feet seven inches tall with large bones and weighed one hundred fifty pounds. Not your perfect cultural image, but not fat. To get my mother off my back, I started eating less food; you know, skipping meals and cutting out snacks. Eventually, I was eating only a few crackers at lunch. The very thought of food sickened me. When my weight fell to one hundred pounds, my mother finally decided I had gone too far. The trouble was that I barely had enough energy to breathe, let alone undertake the struggle to get healthy again. It was a long way back.*

*—Sandi, twenty-nine*

For teens with anorexia, the issues are perfectionism and control. Caught in the throes of a skewed body image, these teens become more and more strict with themselves, allowing only the tiniest of morsels to cross their lips. Confronted by perfectionistic expectations everywhere they turn, some teens decide that the only control they have is over their own bodies. Others slowly starve themselves, believing they do not deserve to take up space; their feelings of self-worth are so low that they try to disappear. Anorexia Nervosa and Related Eating Disorders, Inc. estimates that over eight million people suffer from anorexia in the United States. Most develop the eating disorder during their teen years.[7]

Those teens who fall into the binge-purge cycle of bulimia are obsessed with feelings of impulsiveness, loss of control, and being overwhelmed. They constantly battle the urge to eat everything in sight. Then, feeling guilty about their lack of willpower, they purge by vomiting, using laxatives, and/or overexercising. They are captives of this culture's worship of thinness, perfectionism, and control. Teens with eating disorders are trapped in a void of secrets and silence. However, there are symptoms that signal danger to observant parents:

- sleep difficulties

- the yellowing and/or deterioration of the teeth

- complaints of a sore throat

- scar or sore on the index or middle finger (made by stomach acids from constantly inducing vomiting)

- lack of energy

- dramatic weight loss

- skipping meals, avoiding meals with family

- excess hair on face and body

- fainting spells

The medical dangers associated with anorexia and bulimia include:

- anemia

- kidney damage

- liver damage

- rupture of esophagus

- irregular heartbeat and cardiac arrest

- amenorrhea and infertility [8]

Observance of a cluster of any of these symptoms in your teen's health or behavior is a sign that it's time to immediately call the family physician for help.

Teens who develop eating disorders are often bright, talented, and competent. They present a confident facade to the world around them, while they feel hollow, ineffective, and fearful within. There is probably no way we can prevent our teenagers' concerns with how they look or how much they achieve and how well they do it, but we can counterbalance their worries by being the kind of parents they can come to for help with any concern. Regular check-ins about how they are doing, being involved in their activities, setting fair limits and boundaries, and supporting their passions all keep teens in touch with the realities of what they are capable of and what we expect from them. When we talk about our own talents as well as our faults, we help our teens develop realistic expectations and accurate assessments of themselves. Truly seeing their souls by honoring their accomplishments and acknowledging their likes and dislikes supports self-esteem and the feeling of being worthy of love, just because they are, not because of what they can do.

## Solitude and Community

Friendships and love relationships bloom during the landing years. No longer as encumbered with worry about a body-gone-wild as in the falling years, middle teens experience a new confidence and felicity in community. They revel in their newly developed powers of observation, analytical thought, and critical dialogue. Their prayers might include, "Please, never a dull moment!" By this many teens mean, "Don't make me be alone." Even those who are more comfortable with one-on-one friendships than with a crowd may confuse aloneness with loneliness. "Please, don't let me be lonely," is the cultural lament of today.

Being comfortably alone with oneself in solitude serves the middle teen as well as being with one's friends and family. It simply takes practice to appreciate it. Henry David Thoreau wrote, "I have a great deal of company in the house, especially in the morning when nobody calls." Being in solitude does not necessarily mean being inactive, as many of us fear. Many pursuits are deeply enjoyed in solitude—reading, sketching, painting, practicing a musical instrument, dreaming, studying, gardening, jogging—anything that involves the imagination and the feeling life. In solitude teens can be themselves, and anything is possible.

WARNING: Watching television and using a computer are not rejuvenating activities for teenagers. Eliminating them is not necessary, but limiting their use is vital! We may want to believe that "vegging out" in front of the TV is relaxing, educational, and fun. And it is, occasionally. The negative influences far outweigh the positive, however. Consider these facts:

- By age eighteen, children have seen 200,000 violent acts on television.

- An average child sees 20,000 thirty-second commercials in one year.

- The amount of money spent on television advertising aimed at youth in 1995 was $550 million.

- The ratio of young Americans aged 18 to 25 applying to the Peace Corps in 1995 to those applying to appear on MTV'S "The Real World" was one to two.[9]

- Over the last forty years, violent crime committed by adolescents has increased over 11,000 percent.

- Despite the decrease in the relative complexity of standardized tests given between 1960 and 1990, higher-order thinking and problem-solving skills have diminished by 40 percent. Many researchers directly link these decreases with the excessive viewing of television and movies.[10]

- The recent analysis of 4,063 lifestyle interviews conducted with children between 1988 and 1994 indicate a firm correlation between the hours of television watched per day and obesity. The more time children spend in front of the TV, the heavier they tend to be.[11]

*The primary danger of the television screen lies not so much in the behavior it produces—although there is*

*danger there—as in the behavior it prevents: the*
*talks, the games, the family festivals, and the argu-*
*ments through which much of the child's learning*
*takes place and through which his character is*
*formed. Turning on the television set can turn off the*
*process that transforms children into people.*[12]

—*Urie Bronfenbrenner, Department of Human*
*Development and Family Studies, New York State*
*College of Human Ecology, Cornell University*

Called the "net generation,"[13] by Don Tapscott, author
of *Growing Up Digital*, computer use among today's teenagers registers an all-time high. Researchers and critics of
the rush to put computers in every classroom, however,
share doubts with educators who find that computers do
little to help students learn more easily.[14] Alan Warhaftig,
English teacher at Fairfax High School, Los Angeles, California, observed that when teens cruised the information
superhighway, their favorite Internet sites were about cars,
sports, and movies. Mr. Warhaftig remarks, "When you
look at what's coming out of the inkjet printer, it's basically
pictures of Michael Jordan."[15] An even greater concern
among high school teachers is the growing use of Web
sites that offer term papers to students for a small fee. One
student says, "There aren't a lot of original papers that get
written anymore. I just think it's the latest way to be
lazy."[16] Even more threatening, perhaps, is the idea that
home computers are a tool for developing community, to
link people and develop relationships worldwide. Teens of

all ages who face difficulties in personal interactions run the risk of getting lost in virtual reality, vulnerable to pornographic addiction, empty promises of friendship, and depression. The first study on the psychological and social effects of home computer use showed that even limited time online led to high levels of depression, loneliness, and less interaction with family members and friends.[17]

> *The tragic loss of human values and conscience among young people in America may be symptomatic of the malaise of a generation brought up by, entertained by, and increasingly educated by the non-human, conscience-neutral and bloodless media.*[18]
>
> —*Eugene Schwartz, Waldorf educator*

Helping our teens find an equilibrium between solitude and community can be challenging, especially if we, ourselves, have not achieved this balance. Any encouragement toward spending time in solitary activity needs to extend to all family members; otherwise, we fall into the trap of saying, "Do as I say, not as I do," which, as we have already observed, never works! A parent's daily habit of morning meditation or an evening walk with the family dog offers a healthy model for seeking solitude.

> *I play violin and have taken riding lessons for years, and they take a lot of time, but for the most part, my family has a pretty low-key lifestyle. I'm really grateful that we have time to spend together, just hanging out. I'm glad we aren't like most of my friends whose*

*families are so busy they're never home. Oh, I go out with my friends, and all that, but it's nice to know that we don't all have to go rushing off to something every minute of the day.*

—*April, seventeen*

Some teenagers will seek solace in the whirl of community to avoid the painful clamor of their inner world. Although a new confidence evolves during the landing years, middle teens still experience doubts about how to be in relationships, fears about family conflict, and performance pressures. Protecting one from oneself in a group works for a time, but feelings of loneliness, depression, and exhaustion eventually fell an overactive teen. Although solitude is sometimes painful in youth, it is a necessary balm for the soul.

WARNING: Middle teens continue to face the peril of attempting or committing suicide. While girls may attempt suicide more often, boys are at a greater risk of actually succeeding.[19] Too much solitude and getting lost in too much activity are not necessarily danger signs, but as part of a series of behaviors, these tendencies are greater cause for concern. Watch for:

- Decreased appetite

- Change in sleep patterns

- Change in number of friends and frequency of social activities

- Angry outbursts, fearfulness, and touchiness
- Major personality changes
- Frequent physical complaints or tiredness
- Self-destructive behavior
- Preoccupation with death
- Unusual cheerfulness and attitude that everything is great
- Obsessive fear of world destruction
- Irrational, bizarre behavior
- Overwhelming guilt or shame
- Perfectionism and an overly zealous drive to succeed
- Feelings of hopelessness, sadness, or despair
- Giving away belongings
- Talking about suicide

The following organization offers listings of local chapters and support groups, books, publications, and other information about the prevention of suicide and help for survivors:

American Association of Suicidology
4201 Connecticut Avenue, N.W., Suite 310
Washington, D.C. 20008
(202) 237-2280

## Silence and Sound

How fortunate when two generations in a household develop at least a tolerance for each other's taste in music. All too often, bitter family battles are waged over the "noise" or "trash" that the younger generation listens to. Each family must work out for themselves the solutions to differences in musical preferences among family members. One solution is to outfit everyone with a player and earphones; another is to only allow music in certain rooms of the house; while other parents carefully screen and limit their teens' musical selections. The question here is not whether there is music in the home, but when and how much. Again, the family rules must match family needs. One need that is often overlooked is the need of every human being for silence. Some teens may as well have headphones surgically implanted for the constant sound they seem to crave. We must encourage them, however, to spend a *little* time each day in silence, and in this habit, we lead the way. When human beings, especially the young, are constantly bombarded with visual images and mechanical sound, they become dependent upon outside sources for inspiration, leaving little room for the creative workings of the imagination. Waldorf educator Margaret Meyerkort believed that through our imagination comes our capacity to love. Through our imaginations we see the ideal in our beloved, and are able to perceive his or her pure intentions beneath a nonperfect human action. Without this vision we could not love.[20]

*The imagination can and must be trained just as scrupulously as the intellect is schooled to perceive and adhere to truth and reality, and that imagination is one of the eyes through which we can see into the lawfulness, wholeness, and transformations in the universe.* [21]

—*Rita Levenson*

# KEEPING TEENS SAFE

During the landing years, teens search for ways to make their mark in the world. Their desire to belong, their thirst for knowledge, their growing independence, and our allowing them more freedom all make them more vulnerable to influences beyond our control. The limits we set must be clear, negotiable, yet firm; negotiable, because what worked well for the fifteen- to sixteen-year-old may not be appropriate for the seventeen- to eighteen-year-old. Checking in regularly with each other helps keep limits effective. When our teens repeatedly break a family rule, that rule is either too strict and impossible to keep or it is not applicable to the situation. Remember that fences are to keep our children safe and to teach them to develop their own internal boundaries. A conversation about what isn't working and why helps keep trust high and misunderstandings low.

# The Desire to Belong

During these transition years between falling to earth and actually getting on with living life, teens in the middle years develop their "land legs." They become more accustomed to their changing bodies, deep or conflicting emotions, and clearer intellectual vision. Their desire to belong encompasses a wider community, now including not only family and peers but youth coalitions, political parties, and other social action groups.

*I always had trouble with the social part of school, and I never seemed to find where I belonged. There were the jocks and cheerleaders, the skaters, the farmers, and those in debate and theater. Then my school offered a class where you could volunteer in the community and get credit. Like you could work with little kids or old people or the homeless. The group that took the class really jelled, you know; we all had a common desire. We met once a week at our youth support leader's house, and sometimes we had weekend retreats. It was awesome what we talked about. Stuff you don't usually talk about with other people, like what you want your life to mean and how to help others. A time I'll never forget is a peace conference we went to in San Francisco where we met with the Dalai Lama. There were kids there from all over, and here we were sitting in one room together talking about peace inside yourself, between people, and out in the world.*

—*Juliana, seventeen*

Too often teens in the middle years feel abandoned, because we assume they can and want to be left to themselves. Even the most active teen, however, needs something tangible and solid to rely on. Regular family commitments remain the best way to keep teens safe. Being able to say, "My family has this dumb rule that we have to eat dinner together," or "I have a stupid curfew, so I can't come," gives teens an out when they need one. Although most teens won't admit it, they are glad to have a home base and a family that keeps them accountable. Most of us function best with some sort of daily rhythm, and our teens are not exceptions. Being able to depend upon the family gathering each evening for dinner, regular family video nights, musical evenings, watching Monday night football games, or family read-aloud nights offers an oasis of certainty in the midst of the often chaotic life of the middle adolescent. The usual household responsibilities also keep teens tuned in to family needs. Grocery shopping once a week, cooking a Saturday breakfast or a dinner one night a week, vacuuming, laundry, and occasionally baby-sitting for a younger family member are not unrealistic expectations of a fifteen-to seventeen-year-old.

As we know, curfews help keep our teens healthy by ensuring that they get enough sleep, and they also help keep our teens safe. Unsupervised activities during the wee hours are often the ones that get teens in the most trouble. The decision by some communities to enforce a teenage curfew may not decrease crime and vandalism[22], but it offers positive support to families to help keep kids safe. By combining curfews with effective community programs for youth, cities can creatively dispel the image of teenagers as misplaced citizens *and* reduce crime and vandalism. Those who have organized the clean-up and renovation of neglected neighborhoods, where the incidence of theft and destruction of property is high, report an astonishing reduction in violence. The participants in the project come away with a new sense of ownership and protectiveness toward their community.[23]

During middle adolescence there is potentially overwhelming pressure to do and deal drugs, take risks that defy authority, drink alcohol, drive dangerously, smoke, be sexually active, create computer scams, or shoplift.

What do we do if we discover that our honor roll teen is smoking marijuana? Parents have various reactions to their teenagers' drug use. Some shrug and say, "I tried it when I was a kid, and I was fine. What can I do about it anyway?" Others react with alarm, dragging their teen off to the nearest hospital for a urine test, clamping down on curfews, and forbidding certain friendships. Before taking any action, it is important that parents consider whether their teens' drug usage signals a dependency or a rite-of-passage experiment. Surprisingly, Dr. David Feinberg, a child psychologist and addictions expert at UCLA, estimates that only 5 percent of American teenagers habitually use drugs.[24] Many teens report having tried various drugs at least once.[25] Whether or not drug addiction is as prevalent as parents fear, it is a danger that our teens face, and we want them to make wise choices when presented with the opportunity to sample. Teenagers who face the greatest risk of becoming drug-dependent are those trying to deal with low self-esteem, depression, and other brain/chemical imbalances. Heavy marijuana users often seek the drug's help for depression. Those who choose speed and other amphetamines may be dealing with Attention Deficit Disorder, learning disabilities, and other symptoms from chemical imbalances.

Be sure teens know the facts about drugs. Parents should be aware of the danger signs of drug abuse. Drug addiction affects the behavior, personality, and physical appearance of the user and at the first signs of any of these changes in our teens, parents must realize that something is wrong. Be aware of:

- Rapid mood swings from euphoria to depression, withdrawal to hostility

- A change in personality from an energetic and outgoing person to depressed and uncommunicative

- Blaming others to the point of feeling persecuted

- Happy, depressed, hostile, or angry for no apparent reason

- Focused totally on self and must have own way

- Manipulative by blaming others for their problems and finding ways to deflect the consequences

- Unwillingness to discuss important issues

- Withdrawal from family activities, such as family meals and holiday celebrations

- New friends who refuse to meet or speak with parents
- Radically new style in clothes, jewelry, and hair
- Unable to follow family rules, complete household chores, attend school regularly, finish homework assignments, or keep appointments
- Little interest in extracurricular activities, such as clubs, hobbies, sports, band
- Increase in school problems, such as tardiness, absences, drop in grades, suspensions, or expulsion
- Compulsive talkativeness
- Jittery, jerky body movements
- Sudden weight gain or loss
- Fearfulness
- Fatigue
- Dizzy spells, stumbling, shaky hands
- Bloodshot eyes and/or consistently dilated pupils
- Frequent colds, sore throat, coughing
- Chronically inflamed nostrils, runny nose
- Appears run down, lacking in vitality and health [26]

If a pattern of these signs develops, call the Alcohol and Other Drugs Council at (414) 658-8166 for a free consultation, or call a local drug treatment program for information and referrals for help. The best insurance against drug abuse in our teens is to develop a close, active connection with them to help us be aware of any problems they may be having, such as a struggle with depression or learning disabilities. Counseling, proper medication, and other treatment plans to support these problems will narrow the chances of illegal drug addiction. Clear rules about drug use help teens know the limits. Saying, "We hope you don't use drugs," does little to prevent it. Make it clear that no drugs are allowed in the house, on the family property, or in the family car. If we suspect our teens are trying drugs, we must confront them; talk with them about drugs and their allure; call a local drug program for written information; even take them in for a counseling session, if we think that will get our point across. Some parents are resorting to clipping a bit of their teen's hair while she is sleeping and using the new home-testing kits that screen hair samples for the presence of drugs.

*I was heavily into marijuana when I was seventeen, and it caused all kinds of setbacks for me. I graduated late and missed out on a lot of opportunities that my friends took advantage of. I don't want my daughters to go through the same losses I suffered. They know that if I have any suspicions that they are trying drugs, I'll haul them off to the emergency room for a urine test. Just the thought of an embarrassing scene like that is enough to keep them clean. We talk about it all the time, and I know which friends of theirs are into drugs and which aren't. They know not to hang out too much with the active users.*

*—Virginia, forty-five*

Can our teens make safe choices when we are not there to enforce the rules? Yes, they can—if we hold a place for them within the family, where they feel a sense of belonging, no matter what they do. **The greatest insurance against dangerous activities is to know what is happening in the lives of our teens;** to talk, to listen, to expect family participation, to include their friends in family events, to attend their school presentations and functions, to enforce family rules, and to provide opportunities for volunteer service and creative endeavors. It means **being there**.

## Recommended Reading

*Parenting Your Teenager*, by David Elkind, Ballantine Books, New York, 1993. Engagingly written, this guide supports parents as they face the challenge of guiding their teens into maturity.

*Endangered Minds: Why Children Don't Think and What We Can Do About It*, by Jane Healy, Simon and Schuster, New York, 1990. The author skillfully examines why our children cannot think like children in the past.

*The Teenage Liberation Handbook: How to Quit School and Get a Real Life and Education*, by Grace Llewellyn, Lowry House, Eugene, OR, 1991. For teenagers and people with teenagers in their lives, this book offers hope and great ideas for those who question the benefits of a conventional education in traditional schools.

*A Fine Young Man*, by Michael Gurian, Jeremy Tarcher, New York, 1998. Michael Gurian provides a studious guide to the unique needs of adolescent boys.

*School Girls*, by Peggy Orenstein in association with the American Association of University Women, Doubleday, New

York, 1994. Orenstein's candid descriptions of life conditions for girls guide parents to help their daughters overcome the confidence gap.

*Every Parent's Guide to the Law,* by Deborah Forman, Harcourt Brace, San Diego, 1998. A chapter called "Youths in Trouble" is especially informative about juvenile crime, other transgressions, and parental responsibility.

## ENDNOTES

1.  Staley, *Between Form and Freedom*, 92.

2.  Ibid., 93.

3.  Timothy Gower, "America's Hidden Health Crisis," *The Walking Magazine*, May/June 1997, 52.

4.  Arnold E. Andersen, M.D., current research project on eating disorders in fifth and sixth graders, U of Iowa, College of Medicine, Iowa City, Iowa.

5.  Arnold E. Anderson, ed., *Males with Eating Disorders* (Philadelphia: Brunner Mazel, 1990).

6.  Ibid.

7.  ANRED, Inc. (Anorexia Nervosa and Related Eating Disorders), www.anred.com, Hot Line (541) 344-1144.

8.  Ibid.

9.  TV Free America website, http://www.tvfa.org/stats.html.

10. Jane M. Healy, *Endangered Minds: Why Children Don't Think and What We Can Do About It* (New York: Simon and Schuster, 1990), 197-198.

11. Terence Monmaney, "TV Viewing, Childhood Obesity Linked," *Los Angeles Times*, 25 Mar.1998, sec. Al.

12. Urie Bronfenbrenner, "Who Cares for America's Children?" a lecture given at a conference for the National Association for the Education of Young Children, Boston, MA, 1970.

13. Don Tapscott, *Growing Up Digital: The Rise of the Net Generation* (New York: McGraw Hill, 1998).

14. Sandy Banks and Lucille Renwick, "Classroom Computers Remain More Promise Than Panacea," *Los Angeles Times*, Sunday, 8 June 1997, sec. A1–A26.

15. Ibid., A1.

16. Peter Applebome, "On the Internet, Term Papers Are Hot Items," *New York Times*, Sunday, 8 June 1997, front page.

17. Amy Harmon, "Study Links Net Use to Depression," *Contra Costa Times*, Sunday, 30 Aug. 1998, front page.

18. Eugene Schwartz, *Millennial Child* (Hudson, NY: Anthroposophic Press, 1999).

19. Warren Farrell, *The Myth of Male Power* (New York: Simon and Schuster, 1993).

20. Karen Rivers, "Human Values, Television, and Our Children," in *Models of Love, The Parent-Child Journey*, Joyce Vissell and Barry Vissell (Aptos, CA: Ramira Publishing, 1986), 210.

21. Ibid.

22. Raoul V. Mowatt and Bill Romano, "Crime, Curfew: No Link Found," *San Jose Mercury News*, 10 June 1998, sec. 1A.

23. Roland Gilbert and Cheo Tyehima-Taylor, *The Ghetto Solution* (Waco, TX: WRS Publishing, 1994).

24. Sheryl Gay Stolberg, "Parents Turn To Home Tests for Drug Use," *Contra Costa Times*, Sunday, 22 Nov. 1998, sec. A31.

25. Ibid.

26. Alcohol and Other Drugs Council, 1115 56th. Street, Kenosha, WI 53140, (414) 658-8166.

*Part IV:*

*The Living Years—*
*Young Adulthood*

*The chief difficulty Alice found at first
was in managing her flamingo; she succeeded in
getting its body tucked away, comfortable enough,
under her arm, with its legs hanging down, but
generally, just as she had got its neck nicely
straightened out, and was going to give the
hedgehog a blow with its head, it would twist
itself round and look up in her face...and, when
she had got its head down, and was going to begin
again, it was very provoking to find that the
hedgehog had unrolled itself, and was in the act
of crawling away; besides all this, there was
generally a ridge...in the way wherever she
wanted to send the hedgehog to, and,...Alice
soon came to the conclusion that it was
a very difficult game indeed.*[1]

—Lewis Carroll, *Alice's Adventures in Wonderland*

Between the ages of eighteen and twenty-one, our young people achieve the legal rights of adulthood. They can drive and drink and vote. Their capacities for willing, feeling, and thinking are fully functional, making them capable of making decisions and taking action based on clear thinking moderated by messages from their soul. They can now make life decisions, plan, and act. Having these abilities does not mean that they will automatically use them, however; it simply means that they *can*. Indeed, many young adults find that living on earth is much harder than they expected; that to truly live takes risk, courage, and something beyond themselves yet to be discovered.

They are like Parsifal, setting off in search of the Holy Grail, somewhat clumsy, impulsive, and unsure of the goal, yet following an inner compulsion to carve out their own lives on the strength of their own achievements. Like the innocent knight, the young adult is caught between the wasteland and the search for the sacred chalice. The wasteland, as described by T.S. Eliot in his famous poem called *The Waste Land*, and explored by mythologist Joseph Campbell, represents "a land where everybody is living an inauthentic life, doing as other people do, doing as you're told, with no courage for your own life. That is the wasteland."[2] Because he has been taught that knights do not ask unnecessary questions, Parsifal fails to find the Grail on his first visit to the Grail Castle. He follows the old customs of how a knight is *supposed* to behave, ignoring his own instincts to respond to the suffering of the wounded Grail King. The pressures to be successful often push young adults into living a life that is not really their own; making decisions based on what they *should* be doing; choosing what society says that they *ought* to want from life.

The challenge before our children during these twenty-something years is to remain open to the spiritual potentialities that lie within their souls. This is what the Holy Grail represents: a symbol of an authentic life lived on their own terms, following their own dreams, talents, and resources.

The challenge for parents during these years is to enable the relationship of parent to child to transform into one of trust, friendship, and support—refraining from judgment and criticism; offering advice when asked; keeping clear boundaries between assistance and co-dependency; and acknowledging successes and accomplishments. Learning from our grown children can be a tremendous gift when we are open to their explorations.

> *Now that my daughter is into her own life, she teaches me so much. She invited me to go with her to hear her spiritual teacher speak, and I came away with more understanding of her faith, and she is very dedicated. I am so grateful that she includes me in this way.*
>
> *—Anita, mother of Toni, twenty-five*

> *"Oh, I've had such a curious dream!" said Alice. And she told her sister, as well as she could remember them, all these strange Adventures of hers...; and, when she had finished, her sister kissed her, and said, "It was a curious dream, dear...." ...she pictured to herself how this same little sister of hers would, in the after-time, be herself a grown woman; and how she would keep, through all her riper years, the simple and loving heart of her childhood; and how she would gather about her other little children, and make their*

*eyes bright and eager with many a strange tale, perhaps even with the dream of Wonderland of long ago; and how she would feel with all their simple sorrows, and find a pleasure in all their simple joys, remembering her own childlife, and the happy summer days.* [3]

—Lewis Carroll, *Alice's Adventures in Wonderland*

## ENDNOTES

1. Carroll, *Alice's Adventures in Wonderland,* 96.

2. Joseph Campbell with Bill Moyers, *The Power of Myth* (New York: Doubleday, 1988), 196.

3. Carroll, 147-150.

## ⚜ CHAPTER SEVEN ⚜

# Twenty-Something— The Living Years

*My particular inner desire to fly the Atlantic alone was nothing new with me. I had flown Atlantics before. Everyone has his own Atlantics to fly. Whatever you want very much to do, against the opposition of tradition, neighborhood opinion, and so-called "common sense"— that is an Atlantic. . . . I flew the Atlantic because I wanted to. . . . To want in one's heart to do a thing, for its own sake; to enjoy doing it; to concentrate all one's energies upon it—that is not only the surest guarantee of success. It is also being true to oneself.*

—Amelia Earhart

Now our children embark upon a much longer phase of development, and we may look back in surprise that their childhood passed so quickly. While young adults of the past were married with jobs of their own by age twenty, our children delay marriage by living together, postpone having children, and explore who they are by experimenting with schooling and holding various jobs. They may make many starts and stops that frustrate and try the patience and pocketbooks of parents and other family members. It has not been unusual for young people to go away to college and come back home after graduation; to enter college, become confused or disillusioned, drop out, and come home; or to take a job before going to college while living at home. Over the past decade the following attitude prevailed:

> *I'm just out of college. The company I work for has offered to pay for my MBA degree, but I don't know. I don't have any plans. I don't want to be tied down yet.*
>
> *—Marc, twenty-three*

Our twenty-something children, called the Millennial Generation,[1] will be somewhat different from the Generation Xers, whose resistance to rigid or dead-end futures made it difficult for them to commit to anything long term—college, career, or relationship. Authors Neil Howe and William Strauss predict that our young adults will be more confident in their choices and more inclined to make and follow long-term plans for their futures.[2] According to Howe and Strauss, the Millennials are the most "coached" generation in American history.[3] (Consider the number of coaches our children have had while playing organized sports!) Because we have been so involved in their activities since the day they were born, they will continue to seek our support, advice, and home base.

## Economic Expectations

Those who went through the economic depression of the 1930s expected life to be hard; holding down two jobs to pay the bills was commonplace. Everyone dreamed of a better deal, but the daily struggle was real, and most hung grimly on. The boom of the postwar years raised public spirits, as well as income, and there was a surge in the ability to acquire the "good(s) things in life." The "more is better" trend hasn't slowed since. Our young people begin their twenty-something years from the disadvantaged place of believing that they should be able to step out into the world on the same economic level to which they have been accustomed in their family home. Choosing between going out to dinner and paying the utilities bill may come as a big shock. Not that they are irresponsible or frivolous, perhaps simply inexperienced about the economics of living. Some have even worked their way through college, but when it comes to living out in the real world, they struggle with the ambiguities of working at a job while trying to live an authentic life. It is the search for the Grail pitted against the ethics and expectations of a consumer-oriented society.

Complicating their struggle to become independent adults is the unique position we, their parents, are in. Many of us find ourselves not only parenting our children but caring for our own aging parents as well. The dilemma of balancing finances, career, family time, and personal energy is daunting, if not impossible. How do we meet the demands of our jobs, young children still at home, a fledgling adult, and senior family members all needing our care, attention, time, and even financial support? Many of us, guiltily or angrily or both, wish that the monkey in the shape of our still dependent young adult children would get off our backs.

## Personal Expectations

Further complicating the scene for the living years are the personal expectations young adults have for themselves. Without blinking an eye, they tell us that they will have and do it all—find career satisfaction and financial success, marry happily and forever, be closely involved in parenting their children, *and* have time to search for the Holy Grail, to live an authentic life, and attain personal and spiritual fulfillment. Many also are socially concerned, active in their schools and communities to better the lives of those less fortunate than themselves. These young people have created big shoes to fill, and being used to success in their childhoods, most apply themselves wholeheartedly to these commendable goals. When projects don't work out as expected, or jobs or relationships fail, they are not shy about asking Mom, Dad, or stepparents for help.

It is rare when an eighteen-year-old lives on his own. Between the ages of eighteen to twenty-one, it is not uncommon for young adults to share the family home with their parents. This time can be rich and rewarding for both parties, as well as frustrating and painful. Parents used to reining in their frisky teenagers may find their young adults now refuse to take the bit, challenging previous parental authority and rules. The greatest task facing both parents and their young adult children is to allow—and to work for—the transformation of the relationship from one of dependency to one of mutuality.

This new relationship should be based on a commitment that each party has for the other's well-being. Problem solving leans more towards nurturing the connection with each other, rather than over safety issues or to maintain control over behavior. Parents can still give opinions about smoking or drug use and can forbid it in the home, but it is more difficult to dictate our young adult's behavior away from home. Ideally, the young person understands our position on illegal substances, for example, and respects the limits imposed. In this climate a mutual regard for the rights and responsibilities of both parties can develop.

## A Word About Noncustodial Parents and Stepparents

Protecting our children from an absent parent or stepparent is no longer appropriate after our children turn eighteen. They must now deal with these relationships on their own terms. Remaining an impartial listener is crucial when they air their doubts and concerns. But we can no longer hide any unpleasant truths from them or help them set boundaries with their other parents. We must not pry, give advice, or try in any way to manipulate these interactions. This is an invasion of privacy and impedes the development of maturity in adult relationships.

## The Young Adult at Home

What if these new relationships do not develop? What if our twenty-something child continues to need his training wheels when it comes to assuming adult responsibilities? When a young adult still living at home takes advantage of rights and privileges, disregarding the needs of others, the family is stuck in a dependent relationship, potentially causing anger and resentment on both sides. Having the mature capabilities of willing, feeling, and thinking does not insure that our grown children will use them when they are at home with us; they can plan, take action, and make effective decisions only if they choose to exercise these adult abilities. When behavioral expectations are not clear, and/or young adults do not act responsibly, the home environment becomes a potential battleground, chaotic and stifling. Parents may feel that their only alternatives are to put up with the situation or to turn the young person out of the house. And adult children may feel like running away from home, except that now it is called "living on one's own."

Although their chronological age ranks them as adult, for various reasons, some young people may not be able to assume full responsibility for managing their own lives. Emotional or psychological disturbances or chemical imbalances may be the cause. When a person suffers from depression or Attention Deficit Disorder, adult life does not look that appealing; the effort needed appears too great, and the rewards seem too small. Parents may require that the young adult pursue therapy and medical support for his condition in exchange for the privilege to continue to live at home.

As we emphasize throughout our books, everyone develops according to their own time clock, and some are more ready than others to take on the challenges of maintaining life alone. Because of their unique rate of growth, they may just not be ready to make the big decisions about college, career, or future goals. They may need more time before taking off the training wheels of parental control. For some, college life provides an interim experience between the security of the family home and being entirely responsible for one's livelihood. Accommodations, curfews, meals, and a daily schedule are fairly standardized during the early college years, leaving few choices other than whether or not to attend classes or to study. Others elect to spend a year traveling or studying abroad before making choices that affect long-term goals. Some religious organizations send their young people on a mission of devotion for a year, broadening their perceptions and maturing their abilities to deal with life. Certain countries require two years of military service from their young men and women before they begin a career. We agree with some politicians, teachers, and others who advocate a year of social service for American children as preparation for the future. Time spent volunteering in one's home community with senior centers, boys and girls clubs, homeless shelters, town councils, free medical clinics, and so on, offers experience in the work world, teaches valuable skills and gives young adults a sense of vocation and a taste of what they enjoy doing.

## Using the FamilyMind Question [4]

Whatever the situation, the rules for living at home must be clear, and parents and children must cooperate to encourage the young person on her way. A relationship of mutuality is full of give-and-take, compromise, adjustment, honesty, mutual admiration and concern, and getting one's needs met. Asking the FamilyMind question, "What does this family need now including me?" provides access to feelings that may be difficult to share and to hear. Parents may assume we know all there is to know about our adult children—we raised them, didn't we? However, if they have lived away from home for a time, traveled extensively, or been in personal therapy, they will have changed. Even crossing the threshold from teenager to adult when marking another birthday affects who they are.

The FamilyMind question is quite effective for solving disputes, clearing the air, and making agreements with the young adult living at home. All that is required is that each family member be in touch with his or her needs, wants, and wishes. These doorways to the soul offer insights for family decision-making and help build a relationship of mutuality. Any of the many issues facing families with adult children can be aired and resolved for the good of all concerned. Is this list familiar?

- Rent or free room

- College tuition

- Curfews

- Division of household chores

- Meals/food expenses

- Laundry

- Extending courtesy, saying "I'm sorry," using good manners, and working on relationships

- Friends who visit and/or stay the night

- Spending money for personal items, such as cosmetics, haircuts, clothes, entertainment, eyeglasses, condoms, cigarettes, beer

- Pleasure trips

- Drugs, alcohol, and smoking at home

- Use of the family car/gasoline

- Expectations about spending family time together

- Financial support from a divorced parent and how it is to be used

Using the issue of curfews, here is an example of how the FamilyMind question works. With adult children living at home, curfews are agreed upon more often for courtesy's sake, than for safety. Consider this situation:

Josh has decided to live at home while attending the local community college and working at an auto parts store. Because of classes, he works in the evening and on weekends. He closes the store at 9 P.M. and often studies with friends afterwards. He prefers to get home around midnight. Using the question, "What does our family need around Josh's curfew?" family members voiced their needs. Mother: "I sleep so soundly, midnight is no problem for me." Father: "Since I am a light sleeper and get up early, I'd prefer that you used the downstairs shower when you come in late." Younger brother: "Doesn't matter to me." Curfew issues for this family were easily solved.

Things were a little trickier to work out in Debra's family: After completing high school, Debra, nineteen, accepted a modeling position with a large advertising company in a nearby city. She worked long hours and commuted home by train. Her father was firm that she not travel home alone late at night, and her younger sister, with whom she shared a room, complained that her late arrival always interrupted her sleep. Debra's work was important to her, but safety when traveling alone at night was also an issue. The problem was solved when a colleague of Debra's, who lived in the city, offered her a place to stay on nights when her work kept her later than 10 P.M. Debra agreed to call home to let family know whenever this situation occurred.

Sometimes issues and situations arouse intense emotions and are more difficult to solve or to even discuss without instigating blame, criticism, or even violence.

Here is an example:

Eric ran with a rough crowd in high school and after several encounters with the police had been sent to a drug rehab program for six months. He was released into his parents' custody and lived fairly cooperatively at home until he turned twenty. Then began a cycle of missing days at work, sleeping most of the day, breaking his curfew, and coming home drunk late at night. He seemed depressed and stayed withdrawn from family activities. At this point, Eric's parents were confident that he had not broken the house rule about using drugs at home, but they suspected that he was using drugs again. This possibility was especially hard for Eric's mother whose parents had both been alcoholics, and had badly mistreated her during her childhood. Because of Eric's tendency toward violence in the past, his parents decided to ask their family therapist for help, rather than risk confronting him themselves.

⋘ ⋘ *Don* | So often parents want the therapist to offer them a catchphrase, healing words that solve the problem they face with their children without having to take any action. This isn't because they are bad parents. This is because their situation is an extremely difficult one. In Eric's case, both he and his parents made unrealistic agreements that they were unable to keep. Unless the parents take action, they will continue to support their son's problems. They must face why they have not kept their word; why they have not enforced their boundaries. The FamilyMind question for this

**⬧ ⬧ DON** | family is not to work out how this young man can stay at home. The question must focus on how to solve the problem with respect to the son's adulthood and responsibilities. The son is twenty years old; he has broken both the terms of his probation and the agreements he made with his parents. He has been given several reprieves. He must be asked to leave and to figure this out for himself. This outcome is not a failure on the part of the parents. They are providing a rite of passage for their son. The failure would be to allow this bad situation to continue any longer.

In a more common scenario, Janelle, a graduating college senior, sat down with her single-parent mother to discuss her future plans. After studying in Costa Rica for a year, she fell in love with the people and the culture. She hoped to return there to work, but asked if she could live at home to save money while she applied for jobs. Janelle's mother was quite happy to have her daughter share her home for as long as she needed, and the two of them agreed to make some house rules. This is how they worked out some of the issues of their new living situation:

- **Issue:** Should Janelle pay her mother rent?

- **FamilyMind Question:** What does this family need concerning rent?

- **Janelle's needs:** Janelle wants to save as much money as she can for her move to Costa Rica.

- **Mother's needs:** Janelle's mother pays a reasonable mortgage rate on the home that she owns and does not need the extra cash. What she does need is help with supervision, meal preparation, and transportation for Janelle's fourteen-year-old brother when she takes monthly business trips.

- **Solution:** Janelle agreed to accept this task but felt that one weekend per month was not enough in exchange for her room. She offered to also be responsible for meal planning and grocery shopping for the family.

- **Issue:** How will Janelle pay for personal items, such as cosmetics, clothing, entertainment, etc.?

- **FamilyMind Question:** What do Janelle and her mother need concerning Janelle's spending money?

- **Janelle's needs:** Janelle estimates that her personal expenses are approximately $300.00 per month.

- **Mother's needs:** Although Janelle's mother makes a good salary, she has outstanding student loans and medical bills to pay off. She prefers that Janelle take on her own personal expenses.

- **Solution:** Janelle agrees to be in charge of personal items and because she needs to accrue money for transportation to Costa Rica, she decides to find a job that would pay her for at least thirty hours a week.

- **Issue:** Janelle has a boyfriend. Is it permissible for him to spend the night, sleeping with Janelle in her room?

- **FamilyMind Question:** What does this family need concerning sexuality?

- **Janelle's needs:** Janelle wants to spend as much time as possible with her boyfriend before she leaves. He shares an apartment with two other guys without much privacy.

- **Mother's needs:** Janelle's mother also has a close relationship. She has been discreet about her own sexual life, because of her fourteen-year-old son. What effects would her daughter's boyfriend staying over have on her son? How might she talk with him about this matter, as he deals with all of the changes of puberty?

- **Solution:** ?!?!!

## Sexuality Issues with Young Adults

Janelle's mother had not always been comfortable with her daughter's sexuality. Although Janelle had long term-relationships, was cautious, and used effective birth control methods, her mother found it hard to separate Janelle's active sex life with her own painful sexual past. As the mother dealt with her own relationship issues, she became more accepting of Janelle's sexual growth and was able to listen, advise, and inform. She liked Janelle's current boyfriend and supported their connection. But how was she to handle Janelle's request that her boyfriend occasionally sleep over?

Most parents assert that we can accept our young adult's sexual life as a natural part of growing up. Many of us, however, are uncomfortable when confronted with it first thing in the morning when bumping into the guest waiting in line for the bathroom or finding him drinking a cup of coffee in the kitchen. Janelle's situation involves several concerns, so Janelle's mother consulted her brother and sister-in-law for some insight. Her brother was strongly opposed to a guy occasionally staying over when the couple was not married, if it were his daughter. He just wasn't comfortable with the idea. His wife, however, said that for her it would depend upon the young couple themselves. Since Janelle and her boyfriend had been together for two years, seemed to trust and value each other, and respected family rules about courtesy, curfew, and privacy, she had no problems with the arrangement. Janelle's mother agreed. That left the issue of Janelle's younger brother. A school counselor, who had helped Janelle's family in the past, listened to the mother's doubts about the effects on Janelle's brother. He pointed out that the brother might benefit from seeing affection exchanged between a loving couple. Without his father in the house, he had no role models for this kind of intimacy between a man and a woman. If the mother felt good about the relationship between Janelle and her boyfriend, the counselor advised that the brother would be enriched rather than hurt by the arrangement.

Dealing with the sexual lives of our young adult children requires clarity and comfort with our own sexual relationships. Some of us may succumb to the current cultural beliefs that "anything goes," and that we must accept whatever our children want, when we are really against or not comfortable with their behaviors. FamilyMind solutions aim to meet the needs of all concerned, including parents. When we need to draw the line on certain behaviors in our own homes, our assurance and firmness make our decision easier to accept. Offering alternatives that are compatible for all family members helps the young adult feel supported and cared about, rather than being left to solve the problem alone or to swallow a bitter compromise.

When solutions align with family values and needs, members usually feel relieved and able to accept the responsibilities of making the agreement work. When the values of parents and young adults conflict, as in the following story, relationships become more difficult to maintain.

Marguerite, nineteen, lived at home while attending the local community college. Her parents had agreed to provide room and board while she was in school in exchange for household upkeep and extra chores when needed. The agreements seemed practical and positive to all concerned. The parents had high expectations of themselves and Marguerite, relying on their commitments to be honest and trusting. Marguerite, however, had no intention of following through on their agreements. She attended class sporadically for two weeks; then stopped altogether, spending time with old high school friends who worked at the local coffee bar. Her lack of follow-through at home was more difficult to hide. At first she put her parents off by saying that she had too much studying to do the dinner dishes, laundry, and food shopping. Then she made promises, failed to follow through, and contrived various excuses. Her parents gave her time, thinking that she needed to adjust to the demands of school. She continued to fail in her commitments, however, and further damaged her position with her parents by making deals with them for money. At first she asked for small amounts in exchange for washing her father's truck, for example. Not wanting his daughter to go without, Marguerite's father advanced her the money, expecting his truck to be washed later that weekend. Of course, she was always busy on the weekends with no time to do extra chores. By the time Marguerite was indebted hundreds of dollars to her parents, they realized that their agreements were not working. They were frustrated and beginning to feel resentful. So, this is what they did.

They stopped making deals. A deal, such as, "Give me five dollars now, and I'll wash your truck on Saturday," requires a high level of integrity and commitment. Marguerite was not ready for such a transaction. Neither was she responsible enough to be relied upon to wax the kitchen floor for a party that evening. Her parents realized that Marguerite needed guidelines that brought her in closer as a family member, rather than undertaking responsibilities that tended to separate her. For example, she and her mother worked quite well in the kitchen together and enjoyed cooking family meals. When her parents sat in the kitchen after meals, Marguerite was happy to wash the dishes. Her father decided to give his daughter an occasional five dollars as a gift, rather than as a work exchange. His gifts were limited to twice a week and never more than twenty dollars. The cash with no strings attached provided an opening in Marguerite's relationship with her father, and she became more willing to do her share around the house.

Marguerite's parents truly wanted her to go to college but realized that she might not be ready for such a commitment. They were not willing, however, to support her living at home while she spent her time drinking coffee with her friends. As long as she lived at home, she had to either be in school full time or get a job. Marguerite admitted that she had no interest in school, so she found a job as a groundskeeper for a nearby business. The hours and environment suited her quite well. Today, she is unsure of her future, but she feels good about her relationship with her parents and the increase in her ability to make and keep commitments.

## We Want Them to Grow Up, But We Don't Want Them to Leave Home

Most of us have conflicting feelings about the independence of our young adult children. When they leave home to attend college, get married, pursue a career in a new city, or simply move into an apartment with friends or on their own, our feelings range from relief to doubt to worry. Most importantly, our children must know that the world is not designed to catch them when they fall, but they can *always* come home. It is not a failure to need time out and a welcoming space to regroup. The terms for coming home, however, will be based on the principles of an adult relationship, where the commitment must be for the mutual benefit of all involved.

## Completion of Childhood: The Affirmation Phase

What a blessing when we can experience our children's affirmation of life and watch as they create their own unique quest for their Holy Grail. The gradual transformation of the parent-child relationship to one of mutual respect and regard nurtures the bonds of a friendship and an alliance that are rare indeed. Because of the history we share—the pain, sadness, joys, and triumphs—the relationship between parent and adult child carries the potential for caring, support, and an understanding that goes far beyond most other relationships. When parents open to the possibility that our children have something to teach us—no matter what their stage of development—our fear and worry about their success is transformed into wonder and an appreciation for their journey.

When young people feel that they must prove something to us, struggle against our negativity, and guard against our criticism, our relationship becomes poisoned with anger, resentment, and loss of connection. We may wonder why our adult children seldom call or write, rarely visit, and keep their problems and achievements to themselves. If we have all the answers, there is no room for the inspiration of creative thought, the excitement of discovery, the satisfaction of accomplishment, the joy of being alive.

Whether young adults leap right out into their lives, or whether they live at home for awhile, we can learn from their experiences, perhaps even recover some of the dreams we had at their age. Their passion for changing the world has not yet been dampened by the cynicism that comes with job burnout. Their trust in humankind has not been destroyed by too many betrayals. Their dreams are not yet tarnished with too many failures. Allowing ourselves to look through their beginner's eyes at life's possibilities rekindles our own spirit of adventure. We encourage them to explore by requesting, "Tell me more about your idea." We help broaden their thinking when we ask, "Have you considered this?" We possibly provide the only support available when we say, "I'm behind you all the way." Our adult children need us to become fans rather than critics, waystations rather than deadends, and friends rather than adversaries. What greater gifts to send them on their way?

### Recommended Reading

*The Teenager's Guide to the Real World,* by Marshall Brain, BYG Publishing, Raleigh, NC, 1997. This is a jam-packed guide written in a way that an older teen can readily relate to, on everything from how to get a job and why, to how to control your anger. A good read for parents, too.

*The 7 Habits of Highly Effective Teens,* by Sean Covey, Simon and Schuster, New York, 1998. Older teens will appreciate the organization and planning of this easy-to-read book.

*Parenting Teens with Love and Logic,* by Foster Cline and Jim Fay, Piñon Press, Colorado Springs, CO, 1992. The authors' formula helps parents help their teens find answers and establish values of their own.

*The Family Heart: A Memoir of When Our Son Came Out,* by Robb Forman Dew, Ballantine Books, New York, 1994. There is a beautiful message here for every parent, every adult child, and every family.

## ENDNOTES

1. Neil Howe and William Strauss, "The New Generation Gap," *The Atlantic Monthly,* Dec. 1992.

2. Ibid.

3. Ibid.

4. Jeanne Elium and Don Elium, *Raising a Family* (Berkeley, CA: Celestial Arts, 1997).

# CHAPTER EIGHT

# A Parent's Part in Adolescence

*It all adds up to a hard and rapid falling into*
*earthly life, from which no one can escape*
*without a few bruises!*

—Eugene Schwartz

W e agree that no one escapes the teen years
without a few bruises, especially parents! The
birthing of the soul to earth—and that is
what the teen years are all about—demands our focus, clarity, flexibility, humor, maturity, humility, wisdom, and
above all, our love. We, as well as our teens, are meeting
someone we have never met before. This new person tum-
bles to earth with innocent arrogance, making compar-
isons, forming opinions, and rendering judgments with
newly opened eyes. For the first time brain and heart
begin to work together, and parents often bear the brunt
of this struggle to make sense of a new reality. Until now,
our children were secure in their connection to us and to
the world. They were the world, and the world was them.
Suddenly, they become aware of an edge, a separation, a
new perception of inner and outer differences. They begin

to struggle with dichotomy, paradox, and injustice. They long for fairness in a world gone mad. Their small shoes that followed in our parental footsteps grow to seven-league boots, and they may wander far away from what we know as "home." They challenge us with rudeness, truancy, sloth, dyed hair, defiance, tattoos, piercings, smoking, and depression. They are raw with the longing to be independent and the need to belong. They struggle against us as they seek direction, purpose, and meaning.

When we are challenged by our teenage children, we come face to face with our human shortcomings, perhaps more painfully and poignantly than during any other time in our active parenting years. Our own unconscious childhood wounds, unresolved relationship issues, uncontrolled addictions, and ignored personality weaknesses muddy the waters, so to speak, of the stormy adolescent sea we find ourselves in. We must be willing to question whether our intense reaction to our teen's behavior is really a reaction to that behavior or a response to some inner trauma of our own. Am I upset because I found beer cans in the trunk of my teen's car, or does this evidence touch off my own fears about uncontrolled drinking? Do I become so enraged at my irresponsible teen because he or she causes inconvenience, or because I, myself, am reluctant to grow up and accept adult responsibilities? Do I push my teen into close relationships because I still live with the pain of having been a lonely teenager? This chapter offers an exploration into the big issues that adolescence almost certainly dredges up for parents. When viewed as an opportunity for growth, these years provide a sure direction for working on personal difficulties that have plagued us since we were teenagers ourselves. Our teens ceaselessly search for perfection in their parents and in the world around them and are constantly disappointed. If our goal is to try to become perfect, we, too will be continually thwarted in our quest. It is enough that we strive to understand ourselves and our teens. By being vulnerable to introspection, we become more accessible and able parents. If we have not already done so, our children's adolescence *demands* that we get our act together; that we are clear about moral values; that we consider the social impact of our choices; that we have no qualms about the example we provide for living an honorable life.

## Have You Hugged Your Teen Today?

Our only armor in this holy teenage battle for freedom is love—firm, unlimited, and unconditional. Although their behaviors and words push us away, teens long to be held, understood, and safe.

> *It's easy to hug a cuddly four-year-old. A gentle caress of his hair or a back rub always calmed my young son, so that he was ready to go back to his play. When he got older, it didn't occur to me that he still needed my touch, until I heard a nurse lecture about healing and touch in the hospital where she worked. Casually massaging his tight shoulders or scratching his head during quiet moments (when we're not butting*

*heads!) seems to help us stay close, allows my son to be*
*nicer to me, to be softer. We promised to give each*
*other at least one hug a day.*

*—Nan, forty-two*

On the other hand, a new need for privacy often arises, and young teens may become uncomfortable with the forced hug or caress. Boys, especially, shrug off the comfort of a hug, feeling too awkward in a body suddenly overgrown, experiencing unfamiliar, often embarrassing, urges. Some disguise their need for affection under a cloak of anger or indifference. Most waver back and forth between being affectionate and acting gruff or tough. Humor easily diffuses an uncomfortable situation, and tickling, tousling the hair, or playful wrestling often provides the touching that boys need.

## Issues for Mothers with Teenage Boys

Physical issues often emerge for mothers as their sons enter adolescence. When sons become larger than their moms, some mothers may not be comfortable with wrestling or playful tussling. Setting clear boundaries about tickling, jostling, and general roughhousing will help sons know how far they can go with their mothers, and they learn a healthy respect for their newly-acquired strength and size.

*DON* | When I asked a teenage client whether he knew that he scared his mother, a look of amazement crossed his face. He turned to her to check it out,

> and she vigorously nodded her head. His body had grown to football-player size, but he still imagined himself as a little boy.

Because our sons look adult, both mothers and fathers may credit them with greater emotional maturity than they actually have and lean too heavily on them for our own emotional needs. Single moms and mothers whose marriage relationships are lacking may unconsciously look to their sons for the nurturing, understanding, and support that is more appropriate from a mate. Especially after a painful separation or divorce, teenage sons are likely to be overprotective and hesitant to be totally involved in their own relationships for fear of abandoning their mothers to their pain. Rather than being able to assist their sons through this difficult time, some mothers use them as confidential intimates, pouring out their rage against the husband/father and their fear of the future. When mothers overstep the boundaries between parent and teen, they not only tarnish the relationship between a son and his father but jeopardize the mother-son connection as well. Boys whose emotional lives are crippled by needy mothers become resentful, emotionally closed down, and relationship shy. Please do not misunderstand our point. We **are not** saying, "Never show your painful feelings to your son." No matter their ages, sons learn vital lessons about the feeling life from their mothers and other significant women in their lives. We **are** saying that when mothers find support, understanding, and intimacy from appropriate adults, our sons are able to move on in their own healthy emotional development.

## Issues for Fathers with Teenage Boys

Fathers and sons may also experience difficulties with physical boundaries. Sons who are not as athletically inclined as their fathers and wish they were often suffer pressure to be more of a jock than their interests lead them to be. Overly involved fathers would do well to examine their own unfulfilled needs for athletic glory to avoid pushing their sons into miserable experiences of failure or injury. The father who challenges his son's strength against his own to maintain dominance or physical superiority teaches bullying tactics that often backfire when the son reaches his full physical development. Sons who struggle to measure up to their fathers' expectations may have to deal with self-confidence problems and authority issues. On the other hand, fathers who hold healthy control over their own aggressive tendencies provide positive role models for balancing strength with heart. When sons learn from their fathers how to stand their ground and speak the truth with kindness, they learn the life-affirming way of negotiation and FamilyMind thinking; "What do we all need now, including me?" To learn from a father that the physical body is to be used for giving and receiving pleasure rather than to exert power over others is a priceless gift—to society as well as to a son.

## Issues for Fathers with Teenage Girls

Girls in adolescence become more self-absorbed and more conscious than ever of their appearances. They are fascinated by how their looks and behavior affect others and often find their fathers good target practice for their seductive strategies. While some fathers find this experimentation amusing, others are quite alarmed and unsure about how to handle these enticing flirtations. Because a father, stepfather, or grandfather is the first man in a girl's life, how he responds to her developing sexuality deeply influences her realistic self-perception. If he shies away from her or disapproves of her appearance or removes himself from interactions they had previously enjoyed, the girl will interpret these as reactions to something that is wrong with her; that these changes, over which she really has no control, are somehow not acceptable.

## Number One Rule for Fathers with Adolescent Daughters

Never laugh at or tease girls about their appearance: weight, height, hair (color, texture, style), appetite, physical strength, and so on. Girls at this age are extremely vulnerable to critical comments and teasing innuendoes that carry even a hint of judgment or disapproval. Tell her she is beautiful often, in addition to strong, witty, intelligent, funny, thoughtful, sensitive, and so on.

## Number Two Rule for Fathers with Adolescent Daughters

Continue to find events, activities, and interests that you both share and enjoy doing together. A girl needs her father's attention more than ever now, and fathers must insist on remaining active participants in their daughters' busy schedules. Reach for her hand, rather than your wallet, whenever trouble brews between you. Sit down and listen without saying a word.

> *It wasn't until later that I realized I lost my father when I was fourteen, even though he didn't die until I was thirty-two. He was suddenly unavailable whenever I needed him. We were such great buddies, working on outdoor projects, gardening, cutting wood, talking about all kinds of things. He helped me experience the world in a safe, controlled way. Then he became more comfortable giving me money than he was spending time with me, giving me advice or really listening to my questions and concerns. I wondered what terrible thing I had done to lose his interest. I never considered that the terrible thing I had done was simply to grow up.*
>
> *—Eva, forty-four*

## Issues for Fathers with Teenage Girls

Very few fathers talk about or even allow themselves to think about being sexually turned on by their teenage daughters. Many do not realize that being aware of their daughters' developing bodies is totally natural, and that an unexpected arousal during a playful encounter or intense discussion is normal. What is not normal but extremely harmful, perhaps one of the deepest betrayals a father can commit, is acting on those feelings. A young adolescent practices her developing femininity on her father, trusting that he is a safe, reliable source for positive feedback about the self-image with which she experiments. An inappropriate comment or a touch in the wrong place can shatter a young girl's world and leave a jagged chasm in the father-daughter relationship. This rift naturally widens to include a mistrust or fear of all men and colors the development of future positive relationships.

Some fathers are so put off or alarmed by their physical reactions to their daughters that they withdraw, and are no longer available for the fun or support their daughters had relied on. This withdrawal is a tragedy for both fathers and daughters. Girls are deprived of safe male role models, and fathers miss out on actively participating in their daughters' lives. The greatest gift a father can give his teenage daughter is to broaden his understanding of his own nature. The traditional focus of male sexuality has been limited to intercourse and climax. In truth, a man uses his sexual energy to express himself in the world through many forms, including providing for his family, caregiving, being affectionate, taking action, and in all areas of creativity. **A father must be clear about the distinction between sexual acts and sexual expression.** The expression of sexual energy is the essence of a man's being, appropriate in the workplace, community, and with his family. Sexual action is reserved for private moments with a suitable and willing partner. Gordon Clay, men's advocate and advisor to fathers, suggests, "When you hug your daughters, if it feels uncomfortable, continue. If it feels wrong, stop!" "Most fathers," he says, "know exactly what I am saying, and what I mean."[1] Fathers must find ways to express approval of their daughters' approaching womanhood; that they are proud of them; and that they welcome their new development. Through a father's healthy emotional and physical caring, a daughter learns that the male force can be good, loving, direct, kind, caring, and strong. She learns to tell the difference between a man who respects and cares for her and one who wishes to manipulate and take from her. Within the relationship with her father, a girl develops a necessary trust in herself and others. It is a father's responsibility to learn the healthy boundaries between his own sexual nature and his daughter's developing sexuality.

Both mothers and fathers must take their cues about physical displays of affection from their teens. Being careful to respect boundaries of privacy when outside the home and around friends assures our young people that affection shown and accepted at home will not get embarrassingly out of control in public.

## Unresolved Crush Issues for Mothers and Fathers

Earlier, we described the role of the adolescent crush and its function in shaping an adolescent's emotional life. Worship from afar helps nurture the young teen's longing for a heavenly home, for perfection on earth, for true love. The crush aids in the falling into earthly life, the transition between childhood and a harder, perhaps harsher, grown-up reality. During this phase, teenagers need steady, grounded parents to model a creative, fulfilling adult life. Too often, young people have the vicarious experience of how hard adulthood can be through the worry and stress of their parents as they struggle to pay bills, meet career demands, nurture a family, and manage a household. Who wants to leave the magic of childhood behind to enter this world of unending pressure? The adoration of something or someone wonderful (the crush) lifts teenagers out of this daily drudgery, enabling them to escape, for a time, the onerous task of growing up. As teens mature, they gradually see the joys and privileges of becoming adults, as well as the difficulties and responsibilities. They are then able to move on into more realistic relationships where they no longer lose themselves but engage in the inevitable give and take of less than perfect human interactions.

Some adults are stuck in the adolescent crush phase. We do not have to look too deeply to discover a part of ourselves that does not want to grow up; that is still waiting for Prince Charming; that hopes to win the lottery; that wants Daddy to pay off our credit cards; that wants to ride off into the sunset, leaving all our cares behind. When we are stuck in this adolescent phase, we are vulnerable and quite susceptible to "falling in love" with our fantasies, such as an affair, a career, food, alcohol, or other drugs, which take us away from the worry and stress of our routine lives.

The temptation toward distraction, or a desire to escape from it all, grows acute right around the time our children become teenagers. Often the first cause of our discontent is a marriage or partnership gone stale. Amidst the chaos of our daily lives, we lose contact with each other; take each other for granted; channel any leftover energy into what the children need; and just go through the motions of intimacy. We feel unloved, unattractive, lonely, and desperately unhappy. Our mate's bad habits grow to irritating dimensions, and we begin to wonder what attracted us to this unappealing person in the first place. Unconsciously, we are ripe for an affair.

Another reason for our wanderlust is that most of us reach middle age during our teenagers' late adolescence. Their questions, insights, and criticisms bring to light all of our own insecurities, lost dreams, failures, and weaknesses. The question, "Is this all there is to life?" stirs our fears that our real life has passed us by; that we have missed out on something; that a large part of ourselves lies still undiscovered, unappreciated, and unloved. We look for something—or someone—outside of ourselves to rescue us from our hopeless state. Where the early crush provides teens with a soft landing into adult life, the older crush catapults the adult into a distraction from and avoidance of personal business, such as reexamining life goals, dreams, and ambitions; renewing intimacy and commitment with a spouse or life partner; confronting bad habits, addictions, and other personality or emotional difficulties; reevaluating parenting roles and responsibilities; and so on. The most common, and possibly the most harmful mistake parents of teens make at this juncture is to look outside of ourselves for the solutions to our unhappiness, to "fall in love" with the person of our dreams.

By succumbing to a crush in middle adulthood, we adroitly avoid the pain of our present lives. We become caught up in the excitement of being desirable and loved again. We get lost in the possibilities offered by this new relationship and are ready to throw away our old selves without consideration of the effects upon those who depend on us. We fall into a second adolescence: we start working out, lose weight, dress younger, feel a new vigor, and become obsessed with sex. This is much more fun than dealing with personal development issues, BUT at what price? Just at the time when our teens are coming into their own sexual awakening, we go off the deep end, led by the needs of our own libidos, rather than by the needs of our teens for clear models and direct leadership in how to handle the roller-coaster ride of exploding hormones. The muddle we are in renders us useless as guides through the turmoil of adolescent confusion.

Teenagers left on their own to struggle with the strange feelings, disturbing impulses, and confusing choices of adolescence become resentful, angry, disillusioned, and depressed. Parents too involved in the pursuit of our own fantasies often accompany our teens to the principal's office, juvenile hall, abortion clinic, drug rehab program, or family counselor, before we realize that we—and our families—are in serious trouble.

The sad fact is that relationships formed during this kind of crush rarely last. When we become distracted from the real issues of our lives, we take those difficulties with us into the new relationship and play out the same old patterns we were trying to avoid. The very nature of a crush is to fall in love with the person of our dreams, our perfect mate. As most of us have experienced when dreams come true, they usually fail to live up to our expectations of perfection. After time, we discover that Prince Charming snores, that Cleopatra gives orders, and that Cinderella hates housework. The relationship of our dreams is no different from any other human encounter, potentially full of conflict, pain, and emotional hard work. If we feel dissatisfied with our lives, our children's adolescence is the time to get straight with ourselves, facing the inner work necessary to be straight with them.

## Insurance for the Teen Years

The best way to insure healthy teenage children is to keep our marriages, partnerships, and other close relationships in open, loving connection. How we care for ourselves and others, how we face the inevitable conflicts of daily living, how we set personal boundaries with others, how we give and receive affection, and how we express our needs in connection with others all influence our teenagers' development as loving human beings. When they witness our willingness to admit our mistakes, confront our weaknesses, and make amends, they learn the habit of honesty, self-awareness, humility, and the skills to make healthy relationships. How we show kindness and respect to those we love teaches them lessons beyond any advice we might give them. Both single parents and committed couples model how to belong, how to be fair, and how to give and receive love—the primary issues in most teenage struggles.

Relationships need constant fine-tuning, and it behooves partners or friends (in the case of single parents), to occasionally renew their commitments to one another and their reasons for being together. Spend time alone together on a regular basis, even if it's simply snuggling on the couch in front of the fire. Keep learning about connection, feelings, and commitment by reading, taking classes, joining support groups, enrolling in weekend workshops, looking at educational videos, and trying therapy. Learn to understand and to respect individual and gender differences in communication styles and needs for intimacy. Men and women express feelings and desires differently for different reasons, and we each must stretch to truly meet and know our partners as unique people. There is nothing quite as exciting as learning something new about someone we think we have all figured out!

## When Divorce Is the Answer

Unless we work hard at maintaining intimacy with our partner or spouse, it is all too common for couples to drift apart as the years pass. When the connection cannot be recovered, divorce is the usual choice. Divorce never comes during a good time for children at any age, but a divorce during the teen years can be particularly traumatic. Natural changes are happening all too rapidly for the adolescent, and a change as large as a divorce has an enormous impact. We, of course, do not recommend avoiding divorce at all costs, but we do suggest that certain delicate steps can soften the blow for adolescent family members. Here are some guidelines for making the transition:

*Be clear and honest about what is going to happen.* **"Your mother and I have decided that we cannot live together any more. She is going to find an apartment near our home, and you and your sister will live here with me. This is not your fault. We both will always love you, and you will see your mother often." Do not offer choices, such as "You can live with your mother, or you can stay here in our house with me." This puts children between the two people they love and rely upon most in the world, and having to choose one or the other at any age will break their hearts.**

*Be prepared and open to hearing strong feelings and hard questions from teenagers.* Divorce brings about so many losses for teens. The sense they had of themselves as people who belong to particular families with particular parents who live with them is shattered. They may lose their homes, if the primary parent moves. And if they move to new neighborhoods and schools, they lose their friends. These losses cause intense feelings of grief, anger, and fear. Because it is the parents who make the changes that bring about these losses, we usually receive the brunt of our teenagers' anguish. Answer the questions as honestly as possible, respecting personal privacy. Our teens do not need to know the gritty details of our troubles, so keep your feelings to yourself. They may already be painfully apparent anyway.

**Begin therapy** to deal with the personal anger, grief, loss, fear, and the part we played in the failure of the relationship to avoid repeating the same mistakes and negative patterns in a new one. None of us escape uninjured from a divorce, and a skilled and empathetic third person can offer new insight and realistic assessment of our experiences and feelings.

**Allow at least a year to heal from a divorce before committing to a new love relationship.** We can spend this year focusing on personal growth and the needs of our teenagers. Now more than ever, they need reassurance that we will not abandon them; that they were not responsible for our divorce; that we will still hold the rules and boundaries firmly for them; that we will keep our promises to them; that we hold them accountable for their actions in spite of the divorce and their pain; and that we will be consistently involved in their interests and activities.

**If, after a divorce, you do have a new love, never introduce him or her during the first sixth months after a divorce.** Waiting at least a year is preferable. The grieving process takes time and will be different for parents and teenagers.

**Never break a date with teens for a "date" with someone else.** Your teens will either see through a flimsy excuse or find out about the other date from someone else. This is a MAJOR way to lose their trust.

**Avoid including a new love interest in activities that are specially scheduled with teens for at least six months**

**after a divorce.** It is especially difficult for teens when a parent tries to include someone new in family activities too soon. They feel forced to be nice when they feel angry; forced to accept someone new when they have trouble accepting any of our choices and actions; and forced to act normal when life is way out of whack. Do not expect teenagers to ever like this new person. It may take years, and they may never see this person as someone with any authority or influence over them. We strongly recommend that time with teenage children be carefully reserved just for them, to strengthen the bonds of trust and to allow both parents and child to check in with each other. There will be ample time when our teens are elsewhere for us to pursue new relationships, and they will be extremely grateful for our conscious protection of our time together.

## Don't Take Things Too Personally

In our teenager's battle for freedom, both parents and teens confuse trust with love. If we think about it, we realize that our love is a constant force; it is trust that we do not always have. Their trust in us and our trust in them is usually hard won. Humans have to prove that we are trustworthy; we should not have to prove that we are lovable.

> Until my daughter realized that her curfew had nothing to do with how much I loved her, we had a really difficult time. She constantly accused me of wanting to ruin her life, to not allow her any fun, and to come between her and her friends. Finally, I

*got through to her that her curfew was a matter of safety and trust, not one of love. I told her, "As soon as you show me that you are trustworthy, then your curfew can change." It wasn't long then until she started respecting her ten o'clock curfew. She didn't say anything, just waited for me to make a move. After two weeks, I suggested that we try eleven o'clock. By summer we agreed on a one o'clock curfew on weekends, and she is very consistent in keeping it, unless something happens to delay her, and then she always calls me. It was a hard lesson, but my daughter discovered that being trustworthy opens all kinds of adult privileges for her. She also knows that whether or not she makes mistakes, I'll always love her.* —Britta, fifty

Another mistake most of us make is to equate love with hate. Fear is the other side of love, and when we fear that our teens do not love us, that they think we are stupid, that we embarrass them, or that we are somehow failing them, we allow ourselves to get entangled in their falling to earth and we slow their descent. We take their critical comments and experimental behaviors to heart, become hurt, angry, or offended, and fear our loss of control. The truth is that we *have* lost control; control in the sense that we know what to expect, know what our teens are thinking, and know how to handle them no matter what they do. The minute we take something personally, we become locked in a power struggle with our teens that goes nowhere but into a downward spiral of blame, judgment, anger, and hurt. And it is so easy to do. Our unconscious thinking goes something like this: "Surely we will be at fault if we do not correct her poor grammar; we will be held accountable for the sloppy way he dresses; we'll be condemned for her weird ideas and wacky theories; we'll be judged negligent if he fails to pass his history class," and on and on. If our child were five years old, these suppositions might be true; young children need constant guidance, direction, and reminders. Teenagers, however, no longer need our continuous vigilance but rather clear rules, boundaries, and space to experiment with who they are and what they believe. Hopefully, their choices will reflect some of what they learned as small children from us. When their enthusiasm carries them over the top of our expectations, however, we are presented with the ultimate lesson in the Buddhist concept of nonattachment.[2]

Nonattachment is not the same as being detached. When we are detached from something, we are unreachable, unimpressionable, and unavailable. These positions are never helpful when parenting teenagers. Nonattachment is also not the same as being unattached. Being unattached creates a sense of non-feeling, separateness, or uncommittedness. Most people do not feel safe with someone who is unattached. Nonattachment is the state of being aware of one's own feelings, being open to another's feelings, and allowing both to exist in the same moment without blame, judgment, or trying to change the other. Being nonattached allows us to see them objectively and remain involved without taking our teens' actions or words too personally. Here are some examples:

## #1

**Teen:** "That stupid teacher. I hate his ass!"

**Common parental response:** "Don't talk like that about your teachers. I'm sure he's doing what's good for you."

**Typical teen reaction:** "Oh, yeah. You just don't understand, Mom. You're like all adults; always siding with...."

**Mom's comeback:** "Well, if you would just...."

## #2

**Teen:** "That stupid teacher. I hate his ass!"

**Nonattached parental response:** "Sounds like you had a bad day at school. What happened?"

**Teen:** "Oh, that stupid Mr. X is so unfair!"

**Nonattached parental response:** "Mr. X, your history teacher?"

**Teen:** "Yeah. He gave a pop quiz today and announced that those who scored less than fifty points will be assigned an extra project to do by the end of the semester. He's so stupid. If you score low on a test, it means you're having trouble anyway, so how does he think extra work will help? He's f_____ed."

**Nonattached parental response:** "I want to hear more about this, but you'll have to clean up your language."

**Teen:** Okaaaay, but he makes me so mad!"

Out of habit most of us respond to our teenager's words before we even understand the underlying message. The parent's response in the first interaction was made from the level of good manners, proper conduct, and civilized behavior—always a point of contention between parents and teens but hardly of concern to this upset high schooler. This superficial level of focus fueled the ongoing litany of teenage authority issues and feelings of being misunderstood. Mother and son fell into the same old argument that completely missed what the son needed; the mother's issues got in the way of real communication and understanding. In the second interaction, the mother reserved judgment, listening for information, while setting clear boundaries about how much bad language she would tolerate. This enabled the son to express what was bothering him and required that he only censor his language, not his feelings.

## #3

**Parent:** "Have you done your homework?"

**Teen response:** "I'll do it later." Or, "Don't ask!" Or, "Yeah." (When it isn't done).

**Common parental response:** "How many times do I have to ask you to get your homework done? You know you have homework every night. Why can't you just do it on your own? Don't you know how important good grades are to get into college?"

**Teen response:** "Get off my back! You're always ordering

me around. Why can't you let me run my own life? College isn't so important."

**Parental response:** "You don't know what you're saying. Of course, college is important...."

**Teen response:** "Mmmmm, mmmmmm." (Obscenities mumbled under her breath.)

## #4

**Parent:** "Homework done by eight, and then I challenge you to a game of dominoes (or let's watch a movie)."

**Teen response:** "Okay." Or, "I'm already done with my homework." Or, "I can't possibly finish by eight!" Or, "Would you mind editing my essay?" and so on.

The third interaction implies a "Big Brother" approach to homework and invokes guilt and defensiveness in teenagers. The direct question, "Have you done your homework?" carries an accusation that sets up a me-versus-you situation. By simply stating the family rule, "Homework is done by eight o'clock, so plan your time accordingly, and then we'll do something fun together," face-saving postures, meaningless lectures, and no-win power struggles are avoided. Parents sidestep getting hooked into guilt-tripping tactics and worst-case scenarios about failing to get into college that have no real meaning for teenage people.

## #5

**Parent:** "Stop fighting with your brother, right now! You know better."

**Teen:** "But, he started it!"

**Parent:** "I don't care who started it. You're older and know better than to fight with him!"

**Teen** (yelling angrily): "He usually starts it. You blame me for everything...."

## #6

**Parent** (to teen): "I know that you do not always start the fights with your little brother. I don't know who started this one, but I want you both to stop it."

**Teen:** "Okay. Thanks for realizing that it isn't always my fault."

It is very easy to hold our teens accountable for certain behaviors simply because they are older than their siblings. Because they look old enough, we expect them to act more responsibly than they really are. Parents with small children know how aggravating they can be to get back at or to get attention from older brothers and sisters. It's too easy—and unfair—to expect the older child to take the blame just because he is older. An understanding word of encouragement from a parent goes a long way in helping a teen be more tolerant of a younger family member. Many parents notice a dramatic decrease in sibling rivalry incidents and more cooperation from their teenagers.

## #7

**Parent:** "Have you been smoking grass?"

**Teen:** "Of course not! What kind of a question is that?"

**Parent:** "Are you telling me the truth? Your eyes are all red, you seem spaced out, and I smell it on your clothes."

**Teen:** "Sure, Dad. Like I'm going to tell you that I'm smoking pot!"

**Parent:** "Well, are you?

**Teen:** "Yeah, sure Dad. Anything you say."

## #8

**Parent:** "You've been acting strangely lately when you come home at night. I've noticed that your eyes are red, your clothes smell smoky, and you seem distracted. What's up?"

**Teen:** "Oh, nothing, Dad. Just busy."

**Parent:** "We have always been truthful with each other, and I hope you know that you can talk to me about anything. These signs, however, make me wonder if you're smoking pot. You know our family rules about that." (Pause)

**Teen:** (No response)

**Parent:** "Just remember, you are not to use drugs or alcohol as long as you live at home, and you will live here until you are eighteen."

We advocate a direct approach when communicating with teens. When we come crashing in with threats and accusations, however, their common response is defense, denial, and distance. This knee-jerk reaction prevents them from asking for our help, whether or not they want to confide in us. By immediately implying that they are doing wrong, we set up an us-versus-them interaction that blocks communication and erodes their trust in our support and assistance. Tiptoeing around the problem is also ineffective, and sometimes there are extenuating circumstances. One teen we know whose parents noticed red eyes and a smoky smell when she came home from a party, was not a smoker herself, but was suffering an allergic reaction to the cigarettes smoked by friends around her. Knowing their daughter to be truthful, this family was able to discuss the problem without damaging their open relationship. On the other hand, if a teen is using drugs, more than words are necessary to help, and it is totally appropriate for parents to become very personally involved. Parents must do everything possible to keep their teens off of drugs.

### #9

**Parent:** "You need a haircut!"

**Teen:** "I've decided to grow it long."

**Parent:** "You look a mess. It's long and stringy and hangs in your eyes."

**Teen:** "You're always criticizing how I look. Can't you back off?"

**Parent:** "How one looks says a lot about the kind of person you are."

**Teen:** "Oh, here we go again, another one of your lectures...."

**Parent:** "I'm just saying...."

**Teen:** "Yeah, yeah."

## #10

**Parent:** "I see you're letting your hair grow."

**Teen:** "No, I just haven't had time for a haircut." Or, "Yes, I need a change." Or, "Yeah, the guys in the band thought I'd look better with it longer."

**Parent:** "I think a change is good, just as long as you keep it clean."

**Teen:** "Oh, Mom!"

At some point, we must relinquish control over how our teens look. Part of finding out who they are involves, literally, trying on different outfits, hairstyles, and postures. This does not mean that we must give them *carte blanche* over their appearance, but it does mean that we must pick our battles carefully. For example, is it more important to draw the line about hair or clothes, or is there more worth in putting our foot down over a pierced tongue? Every parent and teen must resolve differences in opinion about adolescent self-expression. The point is, that if we try to veto all experimentation, we set ourselves up for continuous rebellion. Fortunately, hair grows back, skin repairs itself, and tastes change as our teens mature. If our teens feel a lack of control over their lives—and they most assuredly will—the freedom to adorn or decorate their bodies as they choose, as long as they do not permanently damage themselves, should be their prerogative. Many teens take their self-expression to the outer limits, leaving us confused, angry, even hurt. Much of the time, it is not only our reactions that our teenagers pursue, but those of the world at large. When we ask them why the garish hair, tattoos, and baggy, torn clothing, they have difficulty articulating the reasons. "Because I like it," "It's cool," or a shrug is what we receive as a reply. The underlying meaning of our teens' culture, including music, dance, philosophy, and dress, may have a far greater scope than any of us realize. We are reminded of the Balinese custom of decorating the outside of homes with the fierce and frightening faces of monstrous demons, thus acknowledging the dark, ugly side of nature to insure peace and harmony within. Are our teenagers, through their outlandish, often offensive fads, merely manifesting the "dark side" that our culture so often wants to hide or ignore? When the raging, vicious, violent side of nature goes unrecognized, it can take on grotesque proportions. We learn in the *Star Wars* trilogy, the phenomenal works by George Lucas, that The Force has two sides, the dark and the light. Our existence is full of contradictions, complements, and opposites—dark and light; good and bad; black and white; day and night; birth and death; summer and winter; joy and grief; feminine and masculine; action and quiet. By bringing these archetypal images to our attention, teenage conventions heal by challenging us to understand their underlying meanings. Their ideas and appearance are not calculated, personal attacks against us, but rather a symbolic acting out of what is wrong in our society at large. It is something they are compelled to do as part of the rebellion that marks the struggle to become independent beings.

## Readjust Family Roles to Fit Current Needs

A helpful quality in the parenting of adolescents is flexibility. But, haven't we said all along that consistency is essential in the raising of children? Yes, a rhythmic pattern of daily living provides confidence and a sense of safety. But, if certain routines or roles are ineffective or outdated, i.e. the children (or adults) have outgrown them, it is useless to continue doing what does not work. What follows is an example of how a family with teenagers solved a leadership problem.

> One couple I see in my private practice uses a democratic form of leadership in their home. Both parents provide guidance and discipline equally, although the wife elected to put her career on hold so she could be a stay-at-home mother, while the husband developed his career as an attorney. The

teenage children badger Mom constantly for services, answers, decisions, transportation, and limit-setting. The usual teenage stuff, except that this mother does not easily deal with these demands. She is always exhausted and senses that she has lost her individual self. She feels helpless and angry, and is beginning to resent her husband and children. The solution for this family was for Dad, who loves making decisions, to temporarily take over. The much maligned "just wait until your dad gets home" mode of parenting effectively meets the needs, for now, of the people in this family. Mom remains involved in the daily activities but defers the big problems and decisions to Dad, who enjoys being more closely involved in the day-to-day rewards and challenges of parenting teenagers. This temporary restructuring allows Mom to have her life back.

By being flexible, these parents adopted unpopular roles that worked for them. In other households, single parents must set and enforce the limits, while many couples strive to maintain equal authority and involvement. The point is that politically correct conventions don't always meet the needs of family members, and parents must be creative, imaginative, and flexible to find appropriate and effective solutions.

## Go for the Holy Moments

During the falling to earth phase of adolescence, our

teenagers' purpose in being, their destiny, their soul force, their reason for living, is awakening. As parents witness this birthing, our own longing for meaning in our lives is reawakened. If we are wise, we begin to examine what has substance and significance for us, looking inward for messages from the soul. This pilgrimage towards our innermost self helps us sort through the purposeless obligations, the outdated beliefs, and the buried feelings that render our lives sterile and tedious. By using these insights to answer the FamilyMind question, "What does this family need now, **including me**?" we discover what is missing, why it feels as though we are living someone else's life.

Very often we learn that the simple things hold the most importance for us. What the Spanish call *milagros pequeños*, the little miracles, the holy moments are those times when we feel most understood by another person; when we pause long enough to experience the beauty of a sunset; when we allow ourselves to be awed by something that we pass by every day, like our son's new height, our spouse's soft hair, or the forsythia bush growing along the driveway. Ordering our priorities according to what nourishes our souls and meets the needs of our families allows us true freedom to choose how we spend the special moments of our lives.

*The Guest is inside you, and also inside me;*
*you know the sprout is hidden inside the seed.*
*We are all struggling;*

*none of us has gone far.*
*Let your arrogance go,*
*and look around inside.*

*The blue sky opens out farther and farther,*
*the daily sense of failure goes away,*
*the damage I have done to myself fades,*
*a million suns come forward with light,*
*when I sit firmly in that world.* [3]

—Kabir

## Recommended Reading

*The Tao of Parenting*, by Greta Nagel, Penguin Books, New York, 1998. Within the wisdom of the Tao, the author teaches valuable lessons about ourselves and our children.

*Raising a Family*, by Jeanne Elium and Don Elium, Celestial Arts, Berkeley, CA, 1997. A new concept called FamilyMind enables families to focus on relationship dynamics where everyone's needs are met.

*Feminist Parenting*, by Dena Taylor, ed., The Crossing Press, Freedom, CA, 1994. Sixty-one personal stories share thoughts, successes, muddles, and humor in trying to parent children in a socially conscious way.

*The Shelter of Each Other: Rebuilding Our Families*, by Mary Pipher, Ballantine Books, New York, 1996. Beautifully written, this inspiring account reveals what troubles today's families.

*In Praise of Single Parents*, by Shoshana Alexander, Houghton Mifflin, Boston, 1994. This journey into the lives of single parents highlights both the sunrises and sunsets of raising children alone.

*Reinventing the Family: The Emerging Story of Lesbian and Gay Parents*, by Laura Benkov, Crown Publishers, New York, 1994. This groundbreaking book portrays a society that honors all families created out of commitment, care, and love.

*Two-Part Invention: The Story of a Marriage*, by Madeleine L'Engle, Harper Collins, San Francisco, 1988. The author and her husband provide a wonderfully sensitive model of a special marriage.

*The Partnership Way*, by Riane Eisler, Harper Collins, San Francisco, 1990. A companion volume to *The Chalice and the Blade* offers practical information and exercises to help us create healthier and more satisfying relationships.

*The Girl Within*, by Emily Hancock, Fawcett Columbine, New York, 1989. This wonderful resource supports women to rediscover their authentic identities.

*Mother Daughter Revolution*, by Elisabeth Debold, Marie Wilson, and Idelisse Malave, Addison-Wesley, Reading, MA, 1993. This is a must-read for all mothers, daughters, fathers, teachers, therapists, and activists.

*Fire in the Belly: On Being a Man*, by Sam Keen, Bantam Books, New York, 1991. Keen provides men with a new vision of masculinity involving spirituality and passion.

## ENDNOTES

1. Gordon Clay, phone interview with Don Elium, San Anselmo, CA, 13 Jul. 1993.

2. Geri Larkin, *Stumbling Toward Enlightenment* (Berkeley, CA:

# CHAPTER NINE

# Initiation

*When I was a child, I spoke like a child,*
*I thought like a child, I reasoned like a child;*
*when I became a man, I gave up childish ways.*

—1 Corinthians 13-11

Like Peter Pan, many of us do not want to grow up. We want to continue to believe in fairies; to wade through puddles; to know we can fly! We are afraid that we won't have fun anymore; that life will be all work with no time off for doing nothing. We fail to realize that in holding to childish ways, we become victims of our own destinies. We sacrifice our power to make choices, continually reacting to what happens to us, rather than creating what we want to have happen. Then we wonder why it feels as though we are living someone else's life.

❧ JEANNE | Parents often ask us how to help their teens act more maturely and responsibly. Our answer includes modeling mature behavior ourselves. "But I don't really want to grow up!" protested one mother. "Sometimes I just want to have my way about things." Of course, we all occasionally feel like this. What we do not realize is that this attitude carries over into daily family life. The parent who won't set boundaries and then explodes because he is being taken advantage of is showing immature behavior. The spouse who publicly blames her mate for something she failed to do models irresponsible action. A parent who refuses to apologize after making a hurtful mistake is showing signs of not wanting to grow up.

The demarcation between childhood and adulthood has varied throughout history. Children were children during the Victorian age, for example, but boys became adult with the graduation from short pants to long trousers. Nineteenth-century girls, it seemed, never really became adults. They were taken care of by their fathers until they were old enough to marry, then it was the husband's turn to take care of them. Contemporary children have, by comparison, very long childhoods, the period we call adolescence being a fairly recent phenomenon. The age of twenty-one has been arbitrarily designated as the point of becoming a modern adult. This differs from older, tribal cultures, which strictly defined and upheld adult roles, where the time for "giving up childish ways" was blurred. Our young people have more leeway in prolonging dependency, for example, by being long-term students, rather than entering the work force and creating independent lives.

## What Is an Adult?

What defines an adult in our culture? We asked several "adults" and several children for their opinions. Here are their definitions:

An adult is:

- ...a mixture of freedom, responsibility, and disillusionment. —Janetta, twenty-six

- ...a person past eighteen who takes on certain roles and responsibilities. —Roland, thirty

- ...someone who takes responsibility for their past, present, and future, thereby becoming free to choose them. —Landry, forty-six

- ...anyone over twenty-one. —Torunn, fourteen

- ...somebody big that can take care of you. —Linnie, five

- ...when you can drive, drink, dance, and have kids. —Jake, twelve

- ...my mommy and daddy. —Linda, four

We experience or achieve many firsts along the journey towards adulthood. Indeed, the status of adult implies that we have accomplished these incremental signs of growth: the first tooth, the first smile, the first step, the first word; the first day of school, the first baseball glove, the first report card; the first bra, the first menstruation, the first date, the first kiss, the first tux, the first driver's permit; the first job, the first paycheck, the first house, the first child.

## Rites of Passage

These firsts are marked at appropriate ages by the rites and rituals of passage determined by the religious or social

customs of the participants. Baptism, circumcision, confir-
mation, bat mitzvah, bar mitzvah, graduation, wedding,
memorial service, funeral. Although practices vary, each of
these events contain the necessary sacraments of initiation:
preparation, challenge, recognition, acceptance into the
greater community, support for the future, and celebration. Initiation implies accomplishments that ready us for
graduation into a further stage of development. The participation of family, friends, and community in the rites
and rituals of initiation brings meaning and purpose to
life's passage.

> *We lived together for six years before we decided to
> be married, and I didn't think it would make much
> difference in our relationship. But having family
> and friends witness the ceremony that Jon and I
> wrote, and having them celebrate with us, had a
> very deep impact upon our commitment to each
> other and our lives together. Somehow the public
> acknowledgment and recognition of our union made
> us feel supported in our efforts in a way that we had
> not experienced before.*
>
> *—Marty, twenty-five*

Like the Jewish traditions of the bar mitzvah for boys
and the bat mitzvah for girls and the initiation customs of
other ancient cultures, modern families of various religious
persuasions understand the importance of recognizing the
progression from childhood into adolescence into adulthood. Many create their own observances, ceremonies, or

rituals to help mark the transition into a new stage of rights and responsibilities. The elements of these initiation rites are culled from the stories and myths of ancient cultures, religious practices, ethnic traditions, and popular culture. They vary widely from family to family while sharing the vital components of ritual: a sacred space, ceremonial clothing, special food, significant songs, and meaningful prayers.

## Ancient Stories

*"A boy is born, and the tribe rejoices. The infant spends his first months wrapped snugly on his mother's body. He has no sense of where he ends and she begins. Mother is his universe. He rides on her back as she works; he sleeps with her; he learns to mimic her daily household tasks; he plays at her feet. He will remain unnamed until the tribe understands his nature, but his mother calls him Solee. As Solee grows, he explores the boundaries between himself and his mother, and his world expands to perhaps twenty feet from her. He develops relationships with others in the tribe, especially the one called 'Father.' Father has been nearby since his son's birth and takes an active interest in his development. Although he is involved in tribal business and is often away hunting, he spends as much time as he can with his small son. Under the eyes of his parents Solee grows strong, plays with his friends, and turns mischievous. Soon he*

*grows taller than his mother, and his tricks on friends and adults are more risky and dangerous. He is becoming a problem.*

*Then one day, there is a different air of activity among the women of the tribe. All day they labor to make new shelters. They work long and hard, uninterrupted because the men are away on a hunt. The children are shooed from underfoot, and the older boys are put to work. That night all go to sleep early, exhausted. In the middle of the night, strange shouts and frenzied chants awaken the sleepers. They can see torches lighting the sky, winding their way down the mountain toward the village, borne by wild-looking men. The women and children defend themselves with rocks and spears, but it is useless. The crazy men in masks dripping blood go into each home and take all of the boys who are nine to twelve years old. 'Don't take my baby!' the mothers scream, to no avail. The boys, Solee among them, are gone.*

*They are taken into the hills to a cave where a fierce fire burns. The sounds of drums fill the night and shake the ground. The boys are placed in a circle around the fire. The wild men in the crazy masks dance to the drums. All at once, some mysterious force quiets the drums, and each dancer takes his place in front of one of the boys. Solee is terrified. Knives are pulled. Solee screams with the other boys in panic. Suddenly the masks are removed and the boys scream again, this time in astonishment—Father!—as each sees his father's face emerge from behind the monstrous mask.*

*'Father, why did you do this? Mother was so upset, she could have killed you!' The father responds, 'Son, I had to steal you away. She is not your real mother.' 'What do you mean, not my mother? Are you drunk or something? Enough of this. Let's go home,' says the incredulous Solee. The father replies, 'Don't get me wrong. She is a very good woman, but I will introduce you to your true mother in one year.'*

*The boy, who really has no choice in the matter, resigns himself to living for a year with his father and the elders of the tribe, to be counseled about life and what it means to be a man. His strengths and weaknesses are determined, and he receives a new name that reflects his calling in life, Selu, The Wind Runner. He crafts a shield that symbolizes his unique skills and contributions to his tribe. His skin is scored and permanently dyed to indicate that he has become a man. He is taught how to hunt, to fish, to fight, and to love. He learns to seek guidance from the stories of his ancestors and to honor the life-affirming forces that protect him and his tribe.*

*One day Selu and his father are making arrowheads, and his father says, 'Oh, son. There's one more thing I forgot to tell you. I am not your true father.' 'What? You are not my father? Who are you?' The father replies, 'Don't worry. I am a good man, and in a few months, I will introduce you to your true father*

*and your true mother.' Again, the boy has no choice
but to continue. By now his body has filled out; his
muscles are shaped; his skills are more refined. He has
passed many of the tests required to be a man in the
world of his tribe.*

*One night the boys are told that the next day they
will meet their true mother and true father. They go
to sleep anxious and excited. Before the sun rises, the
eldest male of the tribe is assisted by the other men to
the mountaintop. The boys are roused and told to follow. In this ancient culture the young were protected
because they were the hope for the future, and the old
were honored because they held the life wisdom from
the past. And so it is an elder who says to the boys
with the rising of the sun: 'It is time to meet your
true mother and your true father. Feel the earth
beneath you. See the sky and sun above you. These
are your true parents. Love them and learn their
ways, and they will always support you and guide
you. Now go to the village and take your places as
warriors and hunters. And from this day, depend
only upon your true parents.'*

*A cheer rises as camp is broken, and the boys-
made-men go down the mountain to their village.
Selu sees his mother by the river. His first thought is,
'Oh, no. She's gonna be mad! She hated for me to get
dirty, and look at my skin.' He gazes at the permanent stripe of color that marks him as a man. When
Selu's mother sees her son, she moans hysterically,*

*'My son is dead. My son is dead!' Now the boy thinks, 'Even my mother doesn't know me. I am no longer her son. I am a man.' He takes his place in the tribe and continues to learn while he hunts for, protects, and gives life to his community. Eventually he takes a wife and has children of his own. When his son reaches that difficult age, Selu the father pulls out a mask and heads for the hills in preparation for the making of a man." [1]*

*—Composite profile of boyhood in the early Bronze Age, 3000 B.C.E.*

*"A girl is born and the birth attendants run rejoicing through the stone-paved streets, their high voices announcing the joyous news to the community. The new mother beams at her infant daughter. 'You will be Demena, daughter of Dellia,' she whispers as the midwife assists in the afterbirth. The sacred placenta is caught in the fertility bowl, a work of great beauty, carefully crafted by the expectant mother before the birth. The finely wrought vessel, covered in flowers and snake designs, will be offered to the Earth Goddess in thanksgiving for a safe and healthy delivery.*

*The new father waits nearby, readying the offering he, too, will make to the goddess in thankfulness for the safety of his wife and daughter. To a small bundle of sweet herbs he adds symbols of hope for his daughter's life—the tiny replicas of a loom to symbol-*

ize craftship, a scales for stateship, and a fertility bowl in recognition of his daughter's feminine nature and connection to the goddess. He also adds a coin cut in half to symbolize abundance and the even distribution of wealth, a hank of his own hair as his support for her thoughts and ideas, and a pinch of the dark earth in honor of all things in nature.

The tiny Demena thrives, nestled in the sling carried by her mother and grandmother or in the crook of her father's or grandfather's arm. She is lulled to sleep by the whirring of looms weaving cloth, the rustling of scythes cutting wheat, the low murmur of temple chants honoring the goddess. Around her, Demena sees women and men of all ages together creating a life of harmony and beauty from a deep reverence for all living things. She grows up secure in her worth as a person of her household, who will one day hold an important position in her community; as a maker of the sacred ritual vessels, perhaps, or a shopkeeper, or even a breeder of the fine cattle her grandparents keep.

When the young girl reaches thirteen summers, she enters the Temple of the Moon Goddess with the other girls her age to await her first blood. Here she is attended by the women of her community and taught the secrets of her approaching womanhood. She spends her waiting-time in service to the goddess through meditation, working with her dreams, and washing the sacred vessels and ritual vestments worn

*by those who have been called to serve in the temple.
On the morning of her first blood flow, special prayers
of thanksgiving and rejoicing are offered by the community to welcome Demena into her new womanhood. Her body is decorated in sea blues and greens,
and she is adorned with sacred garments and flowers.
Then she is presented to the throng awaiting her
emergence from the Temple of the Moon Goddess. A
great bull is roasted, and after a banquet in her
honor, Demena assumes her place as a young woman,
invested with feminine strength, life-giving powers,
and the blessings of the goddess to fulfill her destiny as
a full and active member of the community."* [2]

—*Composite of girlhood in the
Early Neolithic period, 5000 B.C.E.*

## Modern Stories

*"When our son turned sixteen, we wanted to ack-
nowledge his achievements and recognize the challenges that await him. We wanted to mark this
important threshold without embarrassing him.
Family friends, whose son was also turning sixteen,
asked to join in, so together we created a challenge
and ritual celebration for our sons. Our boys share
common intellectual interests—computers, chess, and
debate. They both participate in tennis, but are more
at home with numbers and ideas than with physical
activity, so we decided that their challenges should be*

*physical ones. We gave our son Jeff the challenge of creating an herb garden in the corner of our backyard. His design was beautiful—circular with triangular-shaped beds, brick paths, and a fountain in the middle. Then he began to dig. His friend Rex was asked to create a backyard watering system, and he set to work drawing plans and learning about sprinklers and digging implements. They were given a month to complete their tasks, which would be celebrated with a ritual and feast. On that day, everyone wore white and congregated first in Rex's backyard. We cheered as he flipped the switch that started his new irrigation system. We toasted him; his proud father told a humorous story about his son; and we sang his favorite song. Then at the site of Jeff's garden, he gave each of us a sprig of rosemary and led us around the brick paths, naming the beautiful herbs and flowers. He was toasted; I, his mother, read a poem; and we sang his favorite song. The boys then shook hands, and we ended with a meal comprised of both boys' favorite foods. What was remarkable was Jeff's continued interest and pride in his herb garden. He faithfully tends his plants and has even learned to cook with them. The change in both boys is subtle but noticeable—both are taking a more active role as family members."*

*—Judith, forty-five*

*"The mothers at my daughter's Sunday school class met regularly to create a coming-of-age ritual. Most of the girls were not yet menstruating, so we chose to focus on a ritual and celebration, rather than on a class with specific facts about menstruation, birth control, and fertility. On the appointed morning, we met before dawn and led the girls through the dark to a high hill where we greeted the sun with songs and chants from various cultures. Each mother presented her daughter with a special gift, meaningful to the two of them, and then led her daughter into the circle of women. We prepared a meal of fruit and sweet rolls with tea and juice, then the mothers shared stories both funny and poignant about their own experiences of growing up. The gift I received from this joyous occasion was an opening to talk with my daughter about menstruation and the coming development of her body and emotions. I noticed that my daughter seemed comfortable with other mothers in the group, and I was glad to know that she could confide in other women, if she needed to. This was also a chance for me to heal some of the bad experiences I had when my own period started."*

*—Renè, thirty-nine*


*"It was the mothers of my son's scout troop that got this whole thing started. To tell the truth, the fathers weren't really enthusiastic about it, at first. Then, I remembered an experience a friend of mine had with*

*a men's group he belonged to. They spent a weekend in the woods, telling stories and learning to drum, and then this old guy got up and said, 'Now I'm going to tell you how to love a woman.' And I guess he did! My friend said that it was the best thing he had ever heard, and he wished that he had learned it when he was sixteen. So, the fathers of our scout troop had a weekend in the woods with our sons, telling stories of our own teenage feelings, fears, failures, embarrassments, and exploits. My friend came, too, and took the old man's part, giving the best talk on love and sex I've ever heard. The boys sat entranced. My son and I are much closer now, and he is able to ask me more of the important questions about life, relationships, and family."*

*—Bret, forty-eight*

*"My daughter asked to have a special event for her sixteenth birthday. She said to me, 'I want it to be more meaningful than just a party, Mom. Something I'll always remember.' Quite surprised, I asked who she would like to invite, and I was further surprised to hear that she wanted to ask her two best friends and six older women whom she admired and was fond of. 'And you, Mom, because you're the most important person in my life.' Wow! I was blown away by this news. She further asked that we create a ceremony for her on the day of her birthday, keeping it a secret until then. Her friends and I had a*

*wonderful time sharing thoughts and ideas about a special ritual for my daughter. We got permission from a nearby county park to be there before dawn, and on the day of her birthday we led my daughter blindfolded from our house along the long mile to a grove of redwood trees in the heart of the park. There in a circle of candles, we chanted, told stories about my daughter, recited poems, feasted, and welcomed her into the circle of women, each of us pledging to remain active and supportive in her life to come. My daughter has cerebral palsy, and to see her there, beautiful, her eyes shining, in that circle of friends and trees, touched my heart. It was truly a celebration of love and accomplishment."*

*—Judith, fifty*

Each of these stories, both ancient and modern, describes the elements of initiation:

- **A challenge**—completing a project, getting up before dawn, sleeping in the woods, trusting others while blindfolded, being led a long distance.

- **A recognition**—songs sung in one's honor, stories told.

- **A celebration**—a gathering of specific friends and family with special foods, songs, and rituals.

- **An acceptance into the greater whole**—welcomed into the community with a new sense of maturity and belonging because of what has been shared and witnessed.

## Initiation into the Self

The act of initiation crosses a metaphorical threshold. It is a new beginning, a move toward something greater than where we had previously been. For modern teenagers, an initiation ceremony provides a recognition of what they are to become. The potential self is honored and called forth. As we all remember, or perhaps are experiencing with our own teens, those years are painful and confusing. Most of the time, we don't like ourselves very much, and we get a clear message that others don't like us all that well, either. The focus of an initiation is on the possible, the sprouting seed, the apparent goodness within each individual youth. When life with a teenager becomes impossible, it is time for an initiation. This rite of passage can require tremendous effort and courage or can be celebrated quietly in an intimate setting. A special evening meal in the teen's honor with favorite foods, songs, and stories may reassure him that his place within the family is secure, no matter how hard life currently seems to be. Or, a trial of larger impact may be necessary to awaken the dormant self. Certain successful programs for troubled youth involve one to three nights alone in the woods, facing fears—of the dark, of loneliness, of growing up. Others offer rigorous physical challenges of rock climbing or whitewater rafting that require the development of trust in fellow group members. Some teens weather these challenges more gracefully than others, but all come through with a better sense of who they are and a deeper understanding of their strengths and weaknesses. None emerge untouched, and these impressions, like the actual scarring during ancient rites, leave the permanent mark of a new maturity.

Parents are easily lost in the chores and responsibilities of daily living. We too often focus on the problems—on what is not working—and forget to look up, to count the stars, to smell the flowers, to be grateful for what is going well in our lives. An initiation celebration offers an opportunity for parents to recognize the positive, the potential, the gifts, and the talents of our teenagers. This rite of passage requires that we pause to rejoice in the miracle of life that our teens embody and struggle to bring to earth. By respecting their struggle, we give them the courage to carry on, knowing that we support them, every step of the way.

## Recommended Reading

*The Art of Ritual*, by Renee Beck and Sydney Metrick, Celestial Arts, Berkeley, CA, 1990. The authors guide us to create and perform our own rituals for growth and change.

*Boy Into Man: A Fathers' Guide to Initiation of Teenage Sons*, by Bernard Weiner, Transformation Press, San Francisco, 1992. This personal account of an initiation ceremony for boys offers a practical guide to coming-of-age rituals.

*Men and the Water of Life*, by Michael Meade, Harper Collins, San Francisco, 1993 Full of initiatory stories, this book has something for anyone seeking to heal modern adulthood.

*Reclaiming the Menstrual Matrix*, by Tamara Slayton, Womankind Books, Sebastopol, CA, 1995. Order this guide to initiations for girls through Womankind Publishing, P.O. Box 1775, Sebastopol, CA 95473.

*Grandmothers of the Light: A Medicine Woman's Sourcebook*, by Paula Gunn Allen, Beacon Press, Boston, 1991. Filled with inspiring stories about ancient practices, this book is a wonderful resource for anyone who is creating a rite-of-passage ritual.

*The Power of Myth*, by Joseph Campbell, Doubleday, New York, 1988. These words from the master of myth provide a firm foundation in the purpose and power of myth in everyday life.

## ENDNOTES

1. Elium and Elium, *Raising a Son*, 39-41.

2. Elium and Elium, *Raising a Daughter*, 38-39.

# ❧ INDEX ❧

❦

*Visit Jeanne & Don Elium at*
*www.raisingafamily.com*

Printed in the United States
by Baker & Taylor Publisher Services